The Talent Code

Daniel Coyle is a two-time National Magazine Award finalist and a contributing editor to *Outside* magazine. He has written for the *New York Times* magazine and *Sports Illustrated*. His previous books include *The Times* bestseller *Lance Armstrong: Tour de Force*, which won Best Biography in the 2006 British Sports Book Awards. He first wrote about the idea of a talent code in a March 2007 article for *Play*. He lives in Alaska.

'I only wish I'd never before used the words "breakthrough" or "breathtaking" or "magisterial" or "stunning achievement" or "your world will never be the same after you read this book." Then I could be using them for the first and only time as I describe my reaction to Daniel Coyle's *The Talent Code*. I am even willing to guarantee that you will not read a more important and useful book in 2009, or any other year. And if all that's not enough, it's also a helluva good read.'
Tom Peters, author of *In Search of Excellence*

The Talent Code

Unlocking the Secret of
Skill in Maths, Art, Music, Sport,
and Just about Everything Else

Daniel Coyle

BOOKS

Published by Random House Books 2009

2 4 6 8 10 9 7 5 3 1

Copyright © Daniel Coyle 2009

Daniel Coyle has asserted his right under the Copyright, Designs
and Patents Act, 1988, to be identified as the author of this work

First published in the United States in 2009 by Bantam,
an imprint of the Bantam Dell Publishing Group
a division of Random House Inc., New York

First published in Great Britain in 2009 by
Random House Books
Random House, 20 Vauxhall Bridge Road,
London SW1V 2SA

www.rbooks.co.uk

Addresses for companies within The Random House Group Limited can be found at:
www.randomhouse.co.uk/offices.htm

The Random House Group Limited Reg. No. 954009

A CIP catalogue record for this book
is available from the British Library

ISBN 9781847945105

The Random House Group Limited supports The Forest Stewardship
Council (FSC), the leading international forest certification organisation. All our
titles that are printed on Greenpeace approved FSC certified paper carry the FSC logo.
Our paper procurement policy can be found at
www.rbooks.co.uk/environment

Mixed Sources
Product group from well-managed
forests and other controlled sources
www.fsc.org Cert no. TT-COC-2139
© 1996 Forest Stewardship Council

Design by Glen M. Edelstein

Printed and bound in the UK by
CPI Mackays, Chatham ME5 8TD

For Jen

Contents

Introduction 1

PART I. Deep Practice 9
Chapter 1: The Sweet Spot 11
Chapter 2: The Deep Practice Cell 30
Chapter 3: The Brontës, the Z-Boys, and the Renaissance ..54
Chapter 4: The Three Rules of Deep Practice 74

PART II. Ignition 95
Chapter 5: Primal Cues 97
Chapter 6: The Curaçao Experiment 121
Chapter 7: How to Ignite a Hotbed 139

Part III. Master Coaching 157
Chapter 8: The Talent Whisperers 159
Chapter 9: The Teaching Circuit: A Blueprint 177
Chapter 10: Tom Martinez and the $60 Million Bet 196

Epilogue: The Myelin World 205
Notes on Sources 223
Acknowledgments 233
Index 237

The Talent Code

Then [David] took his staff in his hand, chose five smooth stones from the stream, put them in the pouch of his shepherd's bag and, with his sling in his hand, approached Goliath.

—1 Samuel 17:40

Introduction

THE GIRL WHO DID A MONTII'S WORTII
OF PRACTICE IN SIX MINUTES

Every journey begins with questions, and here are three:

How does a penniless Russian tennis club with one indoor court create more top-twenty women players than the entire United States?

How does a humble storefront music school in Dallas, Texas, produce Jessica Simpson, Demi Lovato, and a succession of pop music phenoms?

How does a poor, scantily educated British family in a remote village turn out three world-class writers?

Talent hotbeds are mysterious places, and the most mysterious thing about them is that they bloom without warning. The first baseball players from the tiny island of the Dominican Republic arrived in the major leagues in the 1950s; they now account for one in nine big-league players. The first

South Korean woman golfer won a Ladies Professional Golf Association (LPGA) tournament in 1998; now there are forty-five on the LPGA Tour, including eight of the top twenty money winners. In 1991 there was only one Chinese entry in the Van Cliburn piano competition; the most recent competition featured eight, a proportional leap reflected in top symphony orchestras around the world.

Media coverage tends to treat each hotbed as a singular phenomenon, but in truth they are all part of a larger, older pattern. Consider the composers of nineteenth-century Vienna, the writers of Shakespearean England, or the artists of the Italian Renaissance, during which the sleepy city of Florence, population 70,000, suddenly produced an explosion of genius that has never been seen before or since. In each case, the identical questions echo: Where does this extraordinary talent come from? How does it grow?

The answer could begin with a remarkable piece of video showing a freckle-faced thirteen-year-old girl named Clarissa. Clarissa (not her real name) was part of a study by Australian music psychologists Gary McPherson and James Renwick that tracked her progress at the clarinet for several years. Officially, the video's title is *shorterclarissa3.mov*, but it should have been called *The Girl Who Did a Month's Worth of Practice in Six Minutes*.

On screen, Clarissa does not look particularly talented. She wears a blue hooded sweatshirt, gym shorts, and an expression of sleepy indifference. In fact, until the six minutes captured on the video, Clarissa had been classified as a musical mediocrity. According to McPherson's aptitude tests and the testimony of her teacher, her parents, and herself, Clarissa possessed no musical gifts. She lacked a good ear; her sense of rhythm was average, her motivation subpar. (In the study's written section, she marked "because I'm supposed to" as her strongest reason for practicing.) Nonetheless, Clarissa had become famous in music-science circles. Because on an average morning McPherson's camera captured this average kid doing something distinctly un-average. In five minutes and fifty-four seconds, she accelerated her learning speed by ten times, according to McPherson's calculations. What was more, she didn't even notice.

McPherson sets up the clip for us: It's morning, Clarissa's customary time for practice, a day after her weekly lesson. She is working on a new song entitled "Golden Wedding," a 1941 tune by jazz clarinetist Woody Herman. She's listened to the song a few times. She likes it. Now she's going to try to play it.

Clarissa draws a breath and plays two notes. Then she stops. She pulls the clarinet from her lips and stares at the paper. Her eyes narrow. She plays seven notes, the song's opening phrase. She misses the last note and immediately stops, fairly jerking the clarinet from her lips. She squints again at the music and sings the phrase softly. "Dah dah dum *dah*," she says.

She starts over and plays the riff from the beginning, making it a few notes farther into the song this time, missing the last note, backtracking, patching in the fix. The opening is beginning to snap together—the notes have verve and feeling. When she's finished with this phrase, she stops again for six long seconds, seeming to replay it in her mind, fingering the clarinet as she thinks. She leans forward, takes a breath, and starts again.

It sounds pretty bad. It's not music; it's a broken-up, fitful, slow-motion batch of notes riddled with stops and misses. Common sense would lead us to believe that Clarissa is failing. But in this case common sense would be dead wrong.

"This is amazing stuff," McPherson says. "Every time I watch this, I see new things, incredibly subtle, powerful things. This is how a professional musician would practice on Wednesday for a Saturday performance."

On screen Clarissa leans into the sheet music, puzzling out a G-sharp that she's never played before. She looks at her hand, then at the music, then at her hand again. She hums the riff. Clarissa's posture is tilted forward; she looks as though she is walking into a chilly wind; her sweetly freckled face tightens into a squint. She plays the phrase again and again. Each time she adds a layer of spirit, rhythm, swing.

"Look at that!" McPherson says. "She's got a blueprint in her mind she's constantly comparing herself to. She's working in phrases, complete thoughts. She's not ignoring errors, she's hearing them, fixing them. She's fitting small parts into the whole, drawing the lens in and out all the time, scaffolding herself to a higher level."

This is not ordinary practice. This is something else: a highly targeted, error-focused process. Something is growing, being built. The song begins to emerge, and with it, a new quality within Clarissa.

The video rolls on. After practicing "Golden Wedding," Clarissa goes on to work on her next piece, "The Blue Danube." But this time she plays it in one go, without stopping. Absent of jarring stops, the tune tumbles out in tuneful, recognizable form, albeit with the occasional squeak.

McPherson groans. "She just *plays* it, like she's on a moving sidewalk," he says. "It's completely awful. She's not thinking, not learning, not building, just wasting time. She goes from worse than normal to brilliant and then back again, and she has no idea she's doing it."

After a few moments McPherson can't take it anymore. He

rewinds to watch Clarissa practice "Golden Wedding" again. He wants to watch it for the same reason I do. This is not a picture of talent created by genes; it's something far more interesting. It is six minutes of an average person entering a magically productive zone, one where more skill is created with each passing second.

"Good God," McPherson says wistfully. "If somebody could bottle this, it'd be worth millions."

This book is about a simple idea: Clarissa and the talent hotbeds are doing the same thing. They have tapped into a neurological mechanism in which certain patterns of targeted practice build skill. Without realizing it, they have entered a zone of accelerated learning that, while it can't quite be bottled, can be accessed by those who know how. In short, they've cracked the talent code.

The talent code is built on revolutionary scientific discoveries involving a neural insulator called myelin, which some neurologists now consider to be the holy grail of acquiring skill. Here's why. Every human skill, whether it's playing baseball or playing Bach, is created by chains of nerve fibers carrying a tiny electrical impulse—basically, a signal traveling through a circuit. Myelin's vital role is to wrap those nerve fibers the same way that rubber insulation wraps a copper wire, making the signal stronger and faster by preventing the electrical impulses from leaking out. When we fire our circuits in the right way—when we practice swinging that bat or playing that note—our myelin responds by wrapping layers of insulation around that neural circuit, each new layer adding a bit more skill and speed. The thicker the myelin gets, the better it insulates, and the faster and more accurate our movements and thoughts become.

Myelin is important for several reasons. It's universal: everyone can grow it, most swiftly during childhood but also throughout life. It's indiscriminate: its growth enables all manner of skills, mental and physical. It's imperceptible: we can't see it or feel it, and we can sense its increase only by its magical-seeming effects. Most of all, however, myelin is important because it provides us with a vivid new model for understanding skill. *Skill is a cellular insulation that wraps neural circuits and that grows in response to certain signals.* The more time and energy you put into the right kind of practice—the longer you stay in the Clarissa zone, firing the right signals through your circuits—the more skill you get, or, to put it a slightly different way, the more myelin you earn. All skill acquisitions, and therefore all talent hotbeds, operate on the same principles of action, no matter how different they may appear to us. As Dr. George Bartzokis, a UCLA neurologist and myelin researcher, put it, "All skills, all language, all music, all movements, are made of living circuits, and all circuits grow according to certain rules."

In the coming pages we'll see those rules in action by visiting the world's best soccer players, bank robbers, violinists, fighter pilots, artists, and skateboarders. We'll explore some surprising talent hotbeds that are succeeding for reasons that even their inhabitants cannot guess. We'll meet an assortment of scientists, coaches, teachers, and talent researchers who are discovering new tools for acquiring skill. Above all, we'll explore specific ways in which these tools can make a difference in maximizing the potential in our own lives and the lives of those around us.

The idea that all skills grow by the same cellular mechanism seems strange and surprising because the skills are so dazzlingly varied. But then again, all of this planet's variety is built from shared, adaptive mechanisms; evolution could have it no other way. Redwoods differ from roses but both grow through photosynthesis. Elephants differ from amoebas but both use the same cellular mechanism to convert food into energy. Tennis players, singers, and painters don't seem to have much in common but they all get better by gradually improving timing and speed and accuracy, by honing neural circuitry, by obeying the rules of the talent code—in short, by growing more myelin.

This book is divided into three parts—deep practice, ignition, and master coaching—which correspond to the three basic elements of the talent code. Each element is useful on its own, but their convergence is the key to creating skill. Remove one, and the process slows. Combine them, even for six minutes, and things begin to change.

I

Deep Practice

Chapter 1

The Sweet Spot

You will become clever through your mistakes.
—German proverb

CHICKEN-WIRE HARVARDS

In December 2006 I began visiting tiny places that produce
Everest-size amounts of talent.* My journey began at a ram-
shackle tennis court in Moscow, and over the next fourteen
months it took me to a soccer field in São Paolo, Brazil, a vocal
studio in Dallas, Texas, an inner-city school in San Jose, California, a run-down music academy in New York's Adirondacks,
a baseball-mad island in the Caribbean, and a handful of other
places so small, humble, and titanically accomplished that a
friend dubbed them "the chicken-wire Harvards."

---

* The word *talent* can be vague and loaded with slippery overtones about potential, particularly when it comes to young people—research shows that being a prodigy is an unreliable indicator of long-term success (see page 223). In the interest of clarity, we'll
define *talent* in its strictest sense: the possession of repeatable skills that don't depend on
physical size (sorry, jockeys and NFL linemen).

Undertaking the journey presented me with a few challenges, the first of which was to explain it to my wife and four young kids in as logical (read: un-harebrained) a way as possible. So I decided to frame it as a Great Expedition, sort of like those undertaken by nineteenth-century naturalists. I made straight-faced comparisons between my trip and Charles Darwin's voyage aboard the *Beagle;* I sagely expounded how small, isolated places magnify larger patterns and forces, sort of like petri dishes. These explanations seemed to work—at least for a moment.

"Daddy's going on a treasure hunt," I overheard my ten-year-old daughter Katie patiently explain to her younger sisters. "You know, like at a birthday party."

A treasure hunt, a birthday—actually that wasn't too far off. The nine hotbeds I visited shared almost nothing except the happy unlikeliness of their existence. Each was a statistical impossibility, a mouse that had not only roared but that had somehow come to rule the forest. But how?

The first clue arrived in the form of an unexpected pattern. When I started visiting talent hotbeds, I expected to be dazzled. I expected to witness world-class speed, power, and grace. Those expectations were met and exceeded—about half the time. For that half of the time, being in a talent hotbed felt like standing amid a herd of running deer: everything moved faster and more fluently than in everyday life. (You haven't had your ego truly tested until an eight-year-old takes pity on you on the tennis court.)

But that was only half of the time. During the other half I witnessed something very different: moments of slow, fitful struggle, rather like what I'd seen on the Clarissa video. It was as if the herd of deer suddenly encountered a hillside coated with ice. They slammed to a halt; they stopped, looked, and thought carefully before taking each step. Making progress became a matter of small failures, a rhythmic pattern of botches, as well as something else: a shared facial expression. Their taut, intense squint caused them to take on (I know this sounds weird) an unaccountable resemblance to Clint Eastwood.

Meet Brunio. He's eleven years old, working on a new soccer move on a concrete playground in São Paolo, Brazil. He moves slowly, feeling the ball roll beneath the sole of his cheap sneaker. He is trying to learn the *elastico,* a ball-handling maneuver in which he nudges the ball with the outside of his foot, then quickly swings his foot around the ball to flick it the opposite direction with his instep. Done properly, the move gives the viewer the impression that the player has the ball on a rubber band. The first time we watch Brunio try the move, he fails, then stops and thinks. He does it again more slowly and fails again—the ball squirts away. He stops and thinks again. He does it even more slowly, breaking the move down to its component parts—*this, this,* and *that.* His face is taut; his eyes are so focused, they look like they're somewhere else. Then something clicks: he starts nailing the move.

Meet Jennie. She's twenty-four years old, and she's in a cramped Dallas vocal studio working on the chorus of a pop song called "Running Out of Time." She is trying to hit the big finish, in which she turns the word *time* into a waterfall of notes. She tries it, screws up, stops, and thinks, then sings it again at a much slower speed. Each time she misses a note, she stops and returns to the beginning, or to the spot where she missed. Jennie sings and stops, sings and stops. Then all of a sudden, she gets it. The pieces snap into place. The sixth time through, Jennie sings the measure perfectly.

When we see people practice effectively, we usually describe it with words like *willpower* or *concentration* or *focus.* But those words don't quite fit, because they don't capture the ice-climbing particularity of the event. The people inside the talent hotbeds are engaged in an activity that seems, on the face of it, strange and surprising. They are seeking out the slippery hills. Like Clarissa, they are purposely operating at the edges of their ability, so they will screw up. And somehow screwing up is making them better. How?

Trying to describe the collective talent of Brazilian soccer players is like trying to describe the law of gravity. You can measure it—the five World Cup victories, the nine hundred or so young talents signed each year by professional European clubs. Or you can name it—the procession of transcendent stars like Pelé, Zico, Socrates, Romário, Ronaldo, Juninho, Robinho, Ronaldinho, Kaká, and others who have deservedly worn the crown of "world's best player." But in the end you can't capture the power of Brazilian talent in numbers and names. It has to be felt. Every day soccer fans around the world witness the quintessential scene: a group of enemy players surround a Brazilian, leaving him no options, no space, no hope. Then there's a dancelike blur of motion—a feint, a flick, a burst of speed—and suddenly the Brazilian player is in the clear, moving away from his now-tangled opponents with the casual aplomb of a person stepping off a crowded bus. Each day, Brazil accomplishes something extremely difficult and unlikely: in a game at which the entire world is feverishly competing, it continues to produce an unusually high percentage of the most skilled players.

The conventional way to explain this kind of concentrated talent is to attribute it to a combination of genes and environment, a.k.a. nature and nurture. In this way of thinking, Brazil is great because it possesses a unique confluence of fac-

tors: a friendly climate, a deep passion for soccer, and a genet-
ically diverse population of 190 million, 40 percent of whom
are desperately poor and long to escape through "the beautiful game." Add up all the factors and—voilà!—you have the
ideal factory for soccer greatness.

But there's a slight problem with this explanation: Brazil
wasn't always a great producer of soccer players. In the 1940s
and 1950s, with its trifecta of climate, passion, and poverty
already firmly in place, the ideal factory produced unspectac-
ular results, never winning a World Cup, failing to defeat
then-world-power Hungary in four tries, showing few of the
dazzling improvisational skills for which it would later become
known. It wasn't until 1958 that the Brazil the world now rec-
ognizes truly arrived, in the form of a brilliant team featuring
seventeen-year-old Pelé, at the World Cup in Sweden.* If
sometime during the next decade Brazil should shockingly
lose its lofty place in the sport (as Hungary so shockingly
did), then the Brazil-is-unique argument leaves us with no
conceivable response except to shrug and celebrate the new
champion, which undoubtedly will also possess a set of characteristics all its own.

So how does Brazil produce so many great players?

The surprising answer is that Brazil produces great players
because since the 1950s Brazilian players have trained in a particular way, with a particular tool that improves ball-handling
skill faster than anywhere else in the world. Like a nation
of Clarissas, they have found a way to increase their learning

---

* Soccer historians trace the moment to the opening three minutes of Brazil's 1958
World Cup semifinal victory against the heavily favored Soviet Union. The Soviets,
who were regarded as the pinnacle of modern technique, were overrun by the ball-
handling skills of Pelé, Garrincha, and Vavá. As commentator Luis Mendes said, "The
scientific systems of the Soviet Union died a death right there. They put the first man in
space, but they couldn't mark Garrincha."

velocity—and like her, they are barely aware of it. I call this kind of training deep practice, and as we'll see, it applies to more than soccer.

The best way to understand the concept of deep practice is to do it. Take a few seconds to look at the following lists; spend the same amount of time on each one.

A	B
ocean / breeze	bread / b_tter
leaf / tree	music / l_rics
sweet / sour	sh_e / sock
movie / actress	phone / bo_k
gasoline / engine	chi_s / salsa
high school / college	pen_il / paper
turkey / stuffing	river / b_at
fruit / vegetable	be_r / wine
computer / chip	television / rad_o
chair / couch	l_nch / dinner

Now turn the page. Without looking, try to remember as many of the word pairs as you can. From which column do you recall more words?

If you're like most people, it won't even be close: you will remember more of the words in column B, the ones that contained fragments. Studies show you'll remember three times as many. It's as if, in those few seconds, your memory skills suddenly sharpened. If this had been a test, your column B score would have been 300 percent higher.

Your IQ did not increase while you looked at column B. You didn't feel different. You weren't touched by genius (sorry). But when you encountered the words with blank spaces, something both imperceptible and profound happened. You stopped. You stumbled ever so briefly, then figured it out. You experienced a microsecond of struggle, and that microsecond made all the difference. You didn't practice harder when you looked at column B. You practiced deeper.

Another example: let's say you're at a party and you're struggling to remember someone's name. If someone else gives you that name, the odds of your forgetting it again are high. But if you manage to retrieve the name on your own—to fire the signal yourself, as opposed to passively receiving the information—you'll engrave it into your memory. Not because that name is somehow more important, or because your memory improved, but simply because you practiced deeper.

Or let's say you're on an airplane, and for the umpteenth time in your life you watch the cabin steward give that clear, concise one-minute demonstration of how to put on a life vest. ("Slip the vest over your head," the instructions say, "and fasten the two black straps to the front of the vest. Inflate the vest by pulling down on the red tabs.") An hour into the flight, the plane lurches, and the captain's urgent voice comes on the intercom telling passengers to put on their life vests. How quickly could you do it? How do those black straps wrap around? What do the red tabs do again?

Here's an alternate scenario: same airplane flight, but this time instead of observing yet another life jacket demonstration, you try on the life vest. You pull the yellow plastic over your head, and you fiddle with the tabs and the straps. An hour later the plane lurches, and the captain's voice comes over the intercom. How much faster would you be?

Deep practice is built on a paradox: struggling in certain targeted ways—operating at the edges of your ability, where you make mistakes—makes you smarter. Or to put it a slightly different way, experiences where you're forced to slow down, make errors, and correct them—as you would if you were walking up an ice-covered hill, slipping and stumbling as you go—end up making you swift and graceful without your realizing it.

"We think of effortless performance as desirable, but it's really a terrible way to learn," said Robert Bjork, the man who developed the above examples. Bjork, the chair of psychology at UCLA, has spent most of his life delving into questions of memory and learning. He's a cheerful polymath, equally adept at discussing curves of memory decay or how NBA star Shaquille O'Neal, who is notoriously terrible at shooting free throws, should practice them from odd distances—14 feet and 16 feet, instead of the standard 15 feet. (Bjork's diagnosis: "Shaq needs to develop the ability to modulate his motor programs. Until then he'll keep being awful.")

"Things that appear to be obstacles turn out to be desirable in the long haul," Bjork said. "One real encounter, even for a few seconds, is far more useful than several hundred observations." Bjork cites an experiment by psychologist Henry Roediger at Washington University of St. Louis, where students were divided into two groups to study a natural history text. Group A studied the paper for four sessions. Group B studied only once but was tested three times. A week later both groups were tested, and Group B scored 50 percent higher than Group A. They'd studied one-fourth as much yet learned far more. (Catherine Fritz, one of Bjork's students, said she applied these ideas to her schoolwork, and raised her GPA by a full point while studying half as much.)

The reason, Bjork explained, resides in the way our brains are built. "We tend to think of our memory as a tape recorder, but that's wrong," he said. "It's a living structure, a scaffold of nearly infinite size. The more we generate impulses, encountering and overcoming difficulties, the more scaffolding we build. The more scaffolding we build, the faster we learn."

When you're practicing deeply, the world's usual rules are suspended. You use time more efficiently. Your small efforts produce big, lasting results. You have positioned yourself at a place of leverage where you can capture failure and turn it into skill. The trick is to choose a goal just beyond your present abilities; to target the struggle. Thrashing blindly doesn't help. Reaching does.

"It's all about finding the sweet spot," Bjork said. "There's an optimal gap between what you know and what you're trying to do. When you find that sweet spot, learning takes off."*

Deep practice is a strange concept for two reasons. The first reason is that it cuts against our intuition about talent. Our intuition tells us that practice relates to talent in the same way that a whetstone relates to a knife: it's vital but useless without a solid blade of so-called natural ability. Deep practice raises an intriguing possibility: that practice might be the way to forge the blade itself.

---

* Good advertising operates by the same principles of deep practice, increasing learning by placing viewers in the sweet spot at the edge of their capabilities. This is why many successful ads involve some degree of cognitive work, such as the whiskey ad that featured the tag line "...ingle ells,...ingle ells...The holidays aren't the same without J&B."

The second reason deep practice is a strange concept is that it takes events that we normally strive to avoid—namely, mistakes—and turns them into skills. To understand how deep practice works, then, it's first useful to consider the unexpected but crucial importance of errors to the learning process. In fact, let's consider an extreme example, which arrives in the form of a question: how do you get good at something when making a mistake has a decent chance of killing you?

EDWIN LINK'S UNUSUAL DEVICE

In the winter of 1934 President Franklin Roosevelt had a problem. Pilots in the U.S. Army Air Corps—by all accounts the military's most skilled, combat-ready airmen—were dying in crashes. On February 23 a pilot drowned when he landed off the New Jersey coast; another was killed when his plane cartwheeled into a Texas ditch. On March 9 four more pilots died when their planes crashed in Florida, Ohio, and Wyoming. The carnage was not caused by a war. The pilots were simply trying to fly through winter storms, delivering the U.S. mail.

The crashes could be traced to a corporate scandal. A recent Senate investigation had exposed a multimillion-dollar price-fixing scheme among the commercial airlines contracted to carry the U.S. mail. President Roosevelt had swiftly responded by canceling the contracts. To take over mail delivery, the president called upon the Air Corps, whose generals were eager to demonstrate their pilots' willingness and bravery. (They also wanted to show Roosevelt that the Air Corps deserved the status of a full military branch, equal to the Army and Navy.) Those generals were mostly right about Air

Corps pilots: they were willing, and they were brave. But in the harsh winter storms of 1934, Air Corps pilots kept crashing. Early on the morning of March 10, after the ninth pilot died in twenty days, FDR summoned General Benjamin Foulois, commander of the Air Corps, to the White House. "General," the president said fiercely, "when are these airmail killings going to stop?"

It was a good question, one that Roosevelt might have directed at the whole enterprise of pilot training. Early pilot training was built on the bedrock belief that good pilots are born, not made. Most programs followed an identical procedure: the instructor would take the prospective student up in the plane and execute a series of loops and rolls. If the student did not get sick, he was deemed to have the capability to become a pilot and, after several weeks of ground school, was gradually allowed to handle the controls. Trainees learned by taxiing, or "penguin-hopping" in stubby-winged crafts, or they flew and hoped. (Lucky Lindy's nickname was well earned.) The system didn't work too well. Early fatality rates at some Army aviation schools approached 25 percent; in 1912 eight of the fourteen U.S. Army pilots died in crashes. By 1934 techniques and technology had been refined but training remained primitive. The Airmail Fiasco, as Roosevelt's problem swiftly became known, raised the question pointedly: was there a better way to learn to fly?

The answer came from an unlikely source: Edwin Albert Link, Jr., the son of a piano and organ maker from Binghamton, New York, who grew up working at his father's factory. Skinny, beak-nosed, and epically stubborn, Link was a tinkerer by nature. When he was sixteen, he fell in love with flying and took a $50 lesson from Sydney Chaplin (half brother of the movie star). "For the better part of that hour we did loops and spins and buzzed everything in sight," Link later recalled. "Thank heaven I didn't get sick, but when we got down, I hadn't touched the controls at all. I thought, 'That's a hell of a way to teach someone to fly.'"

Link's fascination grew. He started hanging around local barnstormers, cadging lessons. Link's father didn't appreciate his interest in flying—he briefly fired young Edwin from his job at the organ factory when he found out about it. But Link kept at it, eventually purchasing a four-seat Cessna. All the while his tinkerer's mind kept circling the notion of improving pilot training. In 1927, seven years after his initial lesson with Chaplin, Link went to work. Borrowing bellows and pneumatic pumps from the organ factory, he built a device that compressed the key elements of a plane into a space slightly roomier than a bathtub. It featured stubby prehensile wings, a tiny tail, an instrument panel, and an electric motor that made the device roll, pitch, and yaw in response to the pilot controls. A small light on the nose lit up when the pilot made an error. Link christened it the Link Aviation Trainer and put up an advertisement: he would teach regular flying and instrument flying—that is, the ability to fly blind through fog and storms while relying on gauges alone. He would teach pilots to fly in half the time of regular training and at a fraction of the cost.

To say that the world overlooked Link's trainer wouldn't be accurate. The truth was, the world looked at it and issued a resounding and conclusive no. No one he approached seemed interested in Link's device—not the military academies, not private flying schools, not even barnstormers. After all, how could you learn to fly in a child's toy? No less an authority than the U.S. Patent Office declared Link's trainer a "novel, profitable amusement device." And so it seemed destined to become. While Link sold fifty trainers to amusement parks and penny arcades, only two reached actual training facilities: one he sold to a Navy airfield in Pensacola, Florida, and another he loaned to the New Jersey National Guard unit in Newark. By the early 1930s Link was reduced to hauling one of his trainers on a flatbed truck to county fairgrounds, charging twenty-five cents a ride.

When the Airmail Fiasco hit in the winter of 1934, however, a group of Air Corps brass grew desperate. Casey Jones, a veteran pilot who had trained many of the Army pilots, recalled Link's trainer and persuaded a group of Air Corps officers to take a second look. In early March, Link was summoned to fly from his home in Cortland, New York, to Newark to demonstrate the trainer he'd loaned to the National Guard. The appointed day was cloudy, with zero visibility, nasty winds, and driving rain. The Air Corps commanders, by now familiar with the possible outcomes of such hazards, surmised that no pilot, no matter how brave or skilled, could possibly fly in such weather. They were just leaving the field when they heard a telltale drone overhead in the clouds, steadily descending. Link's plane appeared as a ghost, materializing only a few feet above the runway, kissed down with a perfect landing, and taxied up to the surprised generals. The skinny fellow did not look like Lindbergh, but he flew like him—and on instruments, no less. Link proceeded to demonstrate his trainer, and in one of the first recorded instances of nerd power trumping military tradition, the officers understood its potential. The generals ordered the first shipment of Link trainers. Seven years later, World War II began, and with it the need to transform thousands of unskilled youth into pilots as quickly and safely as possible. That need was answered by ten thousand Link trainers; by the end of the war, a half-million airmen had logged millions of hours in what they fondly called "The Blue Box."* In 1947 the Air Corps became the U.S. Air Force, and Link went on to build simulators for jets, bombers, and the lunar module for the Apollo mission.

Edwin Link's trainer worked so well for the same reason you scored 300 percent better on Bjork's blank-letter test. Link's trainer permitted pilots to practice more deeply, to stop, struggle, make errors, and learn from them. During a few hours in a Link trainer, a pilot could "take off" and "land" a dozen times on instruments. He could dive, stall, and recover, spending hours inhabiting the sweet spot at the edge of his capabilities in ways he could never risk in an actual plane. The Air Corps pilots who trained in Links were no braver or smarter than the ones who crashed. They simply had the opportunity to practice more deeply.

This idea of deep practice makes perfect sense in training for dangerous jobs like those of fighter pilots and astronauts. It gets interesting, however, when we apply it to other kinds of skills. Like, for instance, those of Brazil's soccer players.

Brazil's Secret Weapon

Like many sports fans around the world, soccer coach Simon Clifford was fascinated by the supernatural skills of Brazilian soccer players. Unlike most fans, however, he decided to go to Brazil to see if he could find out how they developed those

---

* The military's regard for the efficacy of Link's trainers apparently went only so far. Link was permitted to sell hundreds of his devices to Japan, Germany, and the USSR in the years leading up to World War II, creating a situation where both sides in many dogfights were, training-wise, evenly matched.

skills. This was an unusually ambitious initiative on Clifford's part, considering that he had gained all his coaching experience at a Catholic elementary school in the soccer non-hotbed of Leeds, England. Then again, Clifford is not what you'd call usual. He's tall and dashingly handsome and radiates the sort of charismatic, bulletproof confidence one usually associates with missionaries and emperors. (In his early twenties Clifford was severely injured in a freak soccer accident—suffering internal organ damage, kidney removal—and perhaps as a result he approaches each day with immoderate zeal.) In the summer of 1997, when he was twenty-six, Clifford borrowed $8,000 from his teachers' union and set out for Brazil toting a backpack, a video camera, and a notebook full of phone numbers he'd cajoled from a Brazilian player he'd met.

Once there, Clifford spent most of his time exploring the thronging expanse of São Paolo, sleeping in roach-infested dormitories by night, scribbling notes by day. He saw many things he'd expected to find: the passion, the tradition, the highly organized training centers, the long practice sessions. (Teenage players at Brazilian soccer academies log twenty hours per week, compared with five hours per week for their British counterparts.) He saw the towering poverty of the favelas, and the desperation in the players' eyes.

But Clifford also saw something he didn't expect: a strange game. It resembled soccer, if soccer were played inside a phone booth and dosed with amphetamines. The ball was half the size but weighed twice as much; it hardly bounced at all. The players trained, not on a vast expanse of grass field, but on basketball-court-size patches of concrete, wooden floor, and dirt. Each side, instead of having eleven players, had five or six. In its rhythm and blinding speed, the game resembled basketball or hockey more than soccer: it consisted of an intricate series of quick, controlled passes and nonstop end-to-end action. The game was called *futebol de salão*, Portuguese for "soccer in the room." Its modern incarnation was called *futsal*.

"It was clear to me that this was where Brazilian skills were born," Clifford said. "It was like finding the missing link."

Futsal had been invented in 1930 as a rainy-day training option by a Uruguayan coach. Brazilians quickly seized upon it and codified the first rules in 1936. Since then the game had spread like a virus, especially in Brazil's crowded cities, and it quickly came to occupy a unique place in Brazilian sporting culture. Other nations played futsal, but Brazil became uniquely obsessed with it, in part because the game could be played anywhere (no small advantage in a nation where grass fields are rare). Futsal grew to command the passions of Brazilian kids in the same way that pickup basketball commands the passions of inner-city American kids. Brazil dominates the sport's organized version, winning 35 of 38 international competitions, according to Vicente Figueiredo, author of *History of Futebol de Salão*. But that number only suggests the time, effort, and energy that Brazil pours into this strange homemade game. As Alex Bellos, author of *Futebol: Soccer, the Brazilian Way,* wrote, futsal "is regarded as the incubator of the Brazilian soul."

The incubation is reflected in players' biographies. From Pelé onward virtually every great Brazilian player played futsal as a kid, first in the neighborhood and later at Brazil's soccer academies, where from ages seven to around twelve they typically devoted three days a week to futsal. A top Brazilian player spends thousands of hours at the game. The great Juninho, for instance, said he never kicked a full-size ball on grass until he was fourteen. Until he was twelve, Robinho spent half his training time playing futsal.*

Like a vintner identifying a lovely strain of grape, a cognoscente like Dr. Emilio Miranda, professor of soccer at the University of São Paolo, can identify the futsal wiring within famous Brazilian soccer tricks. That *elastico* move that Ronaldinho popularized, drawing the ball in and out like a yo-yo? It originated in futsal. The toe-poke goal that Ronaldo scored in the 2002 World Cup? Again, futsal. Moves like the *d'espero*, *el barret*, and *vaselina*? All came from futsal. When I told Miranda that I'd imagined Brazilians built skills by playing soccer on the beach, he laughed. "Journalists fly here, go to the beach, they take pictures and write stories. But great players don't come from the beach. They come from the futsal court."

One reason lies in the math. Futsal players touch the ball far more often than soccer players—six times more often per minute, according to a Liverpool University study. The smaller, heavier ball demands and rewards more precise handling—as coaches point out, you can't get out of a tight spot simply by booting the ball downfield. Sharp passing is paramount: the game is all about looking for angles and spaces and working quick combinations with other players. Ball control and vision are crucial, so that when futsal players play the full-size game, they feel as if they have acres of free space in which to operate. When I watched professional outdoor games in São Paolo sitting with Dr. Miranda, he would point out players who had played futsal: he could tell by the way they held the

* For a vivid demonstration of futsal's role in developing the skills of two-time world player of the year Ronaldinho, see www.youtube.com/watch?v=6180cMhkWJA.

ball. They didn't care how close their opponent came. As Dr. Miranda summed up, "No time plus no space equals better skills. Futsal is our national laboratory of improvisation."

In other words, Brazilian soccer is different from the rest of the world's because Brazil employs the sporting equivalent of a Link trainer. Futsal compresses soccer's essential skills into a small box; it places players inside the deep practice zone, making and correcting errors, constantly generating solutions to vivid problems. Players touching the ball 600 percent more often learn far faster, without realizing it, than they would in the vast, bouncy expanse of the outdoor game (where, at least in my mind, players run along to the sound-track of Clarissa tootling away on "The Blue Danube"). To be clear: futsal is not the only reason Brazilian soccer is great. The other factors so often cited—climate, passion, and poverty—really do matter. But futsal is the lever through which those other factors transfer their force.

When Simon Clifford saw futsal, he got excited. He re-turned home, quit his teaching job, and founded the International Confederation of Futebol de Salão in a spare room of his house, developing a soccer program for elementary- and high-school-age kids that he called the Brazilian Soccer School. He constructed an elaborate series of drills based on futsal moves. His players, who mostly hailed from a rough, impoverished area of Leeds, started imitating the Zicos and Ronaldinhos. To create the proper ambience, Clifford played samba music on a boom box.

Let's step back a moment and take an objective look at what Clifford was doing. He was running an experiment to see whether Brazil's million-footed talent factory could be grafted to an utterly foreign land via this small, silly game. He was betting that the act of playing futsal would cause some glowing kernel of Brazilian magic to take root in sooty, chilly Leeds.

When the citizens of Leeds heard of Clifford's plan, they were mildly entertained. When they actually witnessed his school in action, they were in grave danger of laughing themselves to death at the spectacle: dozens of pale, pink-cheeked, thick-necked Yorkshire kids kicking around small, too-heavy balls, learning fancy tricks to the tune of samba music. It was a laugh, except for one detail—Clifford was right.

Four years later Clifford's team of under-fourteens defeated the Scottish national team of the same age; it went on to beat the Irish national team as well. One of his Leeds kids, a defender named Micah Richards, now plays for the English national team. Clifford's Brazilian Soccer School has expanded to a dozen countries around the world. More stars, Clifford says, are on the way.

Chapter 2

The Deep Practice Cell

I have always maintained that excepting fools,
men did not differ much in intellect, only in
zeal and hard work.
—Charles Darwin

INSTALLING NATURAL BROADBAND

Deep practice is a powerful idea because it seems magical. Clarissa begins as an average musician and, in six minutes, accomplishes a month's worth of work. A dangerously unskilled pilot climbs into a Link trainer and, within a few hours, emerges with new abilities. The fact that a targeted effort can increase learning velocity tenfold sounds like a fairy tale in which a handful of tiny seeds grows into an enchanted vine. But strangely, the enchanted vine turns out to be something close to neurological fact.

Early in my travels I was introduced to a microscopic substance called myelin.* Here is what it looks like.

---

* I first encountered myelin while working on an article on talent hotbeds for *Play: The New York Times Sports Magazine* and stumbled across a footnote to a 2005 study entitled "Extensive Piano Practicing Has Regionally Specific Effects on White Matter

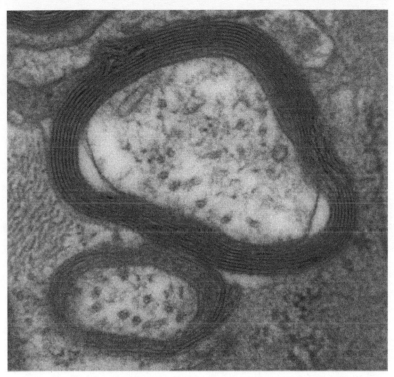

THE STUFF OF TALENT: A cross-section of two nerve fibers being wrapped in myelin. This image was taken early in the process; on some fibers, the myelin insulation grows fifty layers deep. (Courtesy of R. Douglas Fields and Louis Dye, National Institutes of Health.)

One of myelin's side effects is to cause sober-minded neurologists to smile and stammer like explorers who've just stepped ashore on a vast and promising new continent. They don't want to behave like this—they do their best to stay serious and appropriately neurologist-like. But myelin won't let them. Knowing about myelin changes the way they see the world.

Development." I contacted myelin researchers, and within the first ten seconds of the first conversation, I heard a neurologist describe myelin as "an epiphany."

"It's, wow—it's big," said Dr. Douglas Fields, director of the Laboratory of Developmental Neurobiology at the National Institutes of Health in Bethesda, Maryland. "It's early, but this could be huge."

"Revolutionary," Dr. George Bartzokis, professor of neurology at UCLA, told me. Myelin is "the key to talking, reading, learning skills, being human."

Like most people, I was under the impression that the key to learning skills and being human resided in our brain's neurons, that flickering web of interconnected nerve fibers and the famous synapses through which they link and communicate. But Fields, Bartzokis, and others informed me that while they still consider neurons and synapses to be vitally important, the traditional neuron-centric worldview is being fundamentally altered by a Copernican-size revolution. This humble-looking insulation, it turns out, plays a key role in the way our brains function, particularly when it comes to acquiring skills.

The revolution is built on three simple facts. (1) Every human movement, thought, or feeling is a precisely timed electric signal traveling through a chain of neurons—a circuit of nerve fibers. (2) Myelin is the insulation that wraps these nerve fibers and increases signal strength, speed, and accuracy. (3) The more we fire a particular circuit, the more myelin optimizes that circuit, and the stronger, faster, and more fluent our movements and thoughts become.

"Everything neurons do, they do pretty quickly. It happens with the flick of a switch," Fields said, referring to synapses. "But flicking switches is not how we learn a lot of things. Getting good at piano or chess or baseball takes a lot of time, and that's what myelin is good at."

"What do good athletes do when they train?" Bartzokis

said. "They send precise impulses along wires that give the signal to myelinate that wire. They end up, after all the training, with a super-duper wire—lots of bandwidth, a high-speed T-3 line. That's what makes them different from the rest of us."

I asked Fields if myelin might have something to do with the phenomenon of talent hotbeds.

He didn't hesitate. "I would predict that South Korean women golfers have more myelin, on average, than players from other countries," he said. "They've got more in the right parts of the brain and for the right muscle groups, and that's what allows them to optimize their circuitry. The same would be true for any group like that."

"Tiger Woods?" I asked.

"Definitely Tiger Woods," Fields said. "That guy's got a lot of myelin."

Researchers like Fields are attracted to myelin because it promises to provide insights into the biological roots of learning and of cognitive disorders. For our purposes, however, the workings of myelin link the various talent hotbeds to each other and to the rest of us. Myelination bears the same relationship to human skill as plate tectonics does to geology, or as natural selection does to evolution. It explains the world's complexity with a simple, elegant mechanism. *Skill is myelin insulation that wraps neural circuits and that grows according to certain signals.* The story of skill and talent is the story of myelin.

Clarissa couldn't feel it, but when she was deep-practicing "Golden Wedding," she was firing and optimizing a neural circuit—and growing myelin.

When Air Corps pilots deep-practiced inside Edwin Link's trainer, they were firing and optimizing neural circuits—and growing myelin.

When Ronaldinho and Ronaldo played futsal, they were firing and optimizing their circuits more often and more precisely than when they played the outdoor game. They were growing more myelin.

Like any decent epiphany, the recognition of the importance of myelin jolts old perceptions. After I visited Fields and the other myelin scientists, I felt as if I had donned X-ray glasses that showed me a new way of seeing the world. I saw myelin's principles operating not just in the talent hotbeds but also in my kids' piano practicing, in my wife's new hockey obsession, and in my questionable forays into karaoke.* It was an unambiguously good feeling, a happy buzz of replacing guesswork and voodoo with a clear, understandable mechanism. Hazy questions snapped into focus.

Q: Why is targeted, mistake-focused practice so effective?
A: Because the best way to build a good circuit is to fire it, attend to mistakes, then fire it again, over and over. Struggle is not an option: it's a biological requirement.

Q: Why are passion and persistence key ingredients of talent?
A: Because wrapping myelin around a big circuit requires immense energy and time. If you don't love it, you'll never work hard enough to be great.

---

* Also in the skills of a certain Tour de France cyclist. For a previous book, I had spent a year following Lance Armstrong as he prepared for what is widely considered to be the world's toughest race. While the physical demands were unique, there's no question that Armstrong's mental approach—the maniacal focus on errors, the desire to optimize every dimension of the race, the restless eagerness to operate at the edges of his (and everyone else's) abilities—added up to a one-man clinic on the power of deep practice.

Q: What's the best way to get to Carnegie Hall?
A: Go straight down Myelin Street.

My journey down Myelin Street began with a visit to an incubator at the Laboratory of Developmental Neurobiology at the National Institutes of Health. The incubator, about the size of a small refrigerator, held shiny wire racks on which sat several rows of petri dishes containing a pink-Gatorade-looking liquid. Inside the pink liquid were platinum electrodes sending tiny bursts of current to mouse neurons covered with a pearlescent white substance.

"That's it," said Dr. Fields. "That's the stuff."

Fields, fifty-four, is a sinewy, energetic man with a broad smile and a jaunty gait. A former biological oceanographer, he oversees a six-person, seven-room lab that is outfitted with hissing canisters, buzzing electrical boxes, and tidy bundles of wires and hoses, and that resembles nothing so much as a tidy, efficient ship. In addition, Fields has the sea captain's habit of making extremely exciting moments sound matter-of-fact. The more exciting something is, the more boring he makes it seem. For instance, he was telling me about a six-day climb of Yosemite's 3,500-foot El Capitan that he made two summers back, and I asked what it felt like to sleep while hanging from a rope thousands of feet above the ground. "It's actually not that different," Fields said, his expression so unchanging that he might have been discussing a trip to the grocery store. "You adapt."

Now Fields reaches into the incubator, extracts one of the pink petri dishes, and slides it beneath a microscope. His voice is quiet. "Have a peek," he says.

I lean in, expecting to see something sci-fi and magical-looking. Instead I see a tangled bunch of spaghettilike threads, which Fields informs me are nerve fibers. The myelin is harder to see, a faintly undulating fringe on the edge of the neurons. I blink, refocus, and struggle to imagine how this stuff may be the common link between Mozart and Michael Jordan, or at the very least the key to improving my golf game.

Fortunately Dr. Fields is a good teacher, and in our conversations over the previous days he has explained the two principles that underpin an understanding of myelin and skill. Talking to him, as to many neurologists, feels something like mountain-climbing itself: it involves a bit of sweat, but you're rewarded with a new and lofty perspective.

For starters, there's Useful Brain Science Insight Number 1: All actions are really the result of electrical impulses sent along chains of nerve fibers. Basically, our brains are bundles of wires—100 billion wires called neurons, connected to each other by synapses. Whenever you do something, your brain sends a signal through those chains of nerve fibers to your muscles. Each time you practice anything—sing a tune, swing a club, read this sentence—a different highly specific circuit lights up in your mind, sort of like a string of Christmas lights. The simplest skill—say, a tennis backhand—involves a circuit made up of hundreds of thousands of fibers and synapses.

Fundamentally, every one of those circuits looks like this:

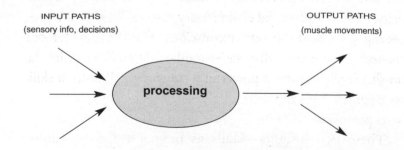

The input is all the stuff that happens before we perform an action: seeing the ball, feeling the racquet's position in our hand, deciding to swing. The output is the performance itself: the signals that move the muscles with the right timing and force to take a step, turn the hips, the shoulders, the arm.

When you hit that backhand (or play an A-minor chord, or make a chess move), an impulse travels down those fibers, like voltage through a cord, triggering the other fibers to fire. The point is that these circuits, not our obedient, mindless muscles, are the true control center of every human movement, thought, and skill. In a profound way the circuit *is* the movement: it dictates the precise strength and timing of each muscle contraction, the shape and content of each thought. A sluggish, unreliable circuit means a sluggish, unreliable movement; on the other hand, a fast, synchronous circuit means a fast, synchronous movement. When a coach uses the phrase "muscle memory," he is actually talking about circuits; by themselves, our muscles are as useful as a puppet without strings. As Dr. Fields puts it, our skills are all in our wires.

Then there's Useful Brain Science Insight Number 2: The more we develop a skill circuit, the less we're aware that we're using it. We're built to make skills automatic, to stash them in our unconscious mind. This process, which is called automaticity, exists for powerful evolutionary reasons. (The more processing we can do in our unconscious minds, the better our chances of noticing that saber-toothed tiger lurking in the brush.) It also creates a powerfully convincing illusion: a skill, once gained, feels utterly natural, as if it's something we've always possessed.

These two insights—skills as brain circuits and automaticity—create a paradoxical combination: we're forever

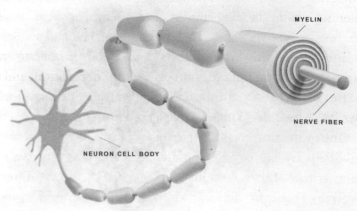

(illustration by Jim Gallagher)

building vast, intricate circuits, and we're simultaneously forgetting that we built them. Which is where myelin comes in.

To say that myelin looks boring is to flatter it. Myelin does not look merely boring. It looks fantastically, unrelentingly, stupendously dull. If the brain is a *Blade Runner* cityscape of dazzling neuronal structures, flashing lights, and whizzing impulses, then myelin plays the humble role of the asphalt. It's the uniform, seemingly inert infrastructure. It's composed of a mundanity known as phospholipid membrane, a dense fat that wraps like electrical tape around a nerve fiber, preventing the electrical impulses from leaking out. It arrives in a series of long, rounded shapes that more than one neurologist unpoetically describes as "sausagey."

Given the seemingly obvious supremacy of neurons, the first brain researchers confidently named their new science neurology, even though myelin and its supporter cells, known as white matter, account for more than half of the brain's mass. For a century researchers have focused their attention on neurons and synapses rather than on their seemingly inert insulation, which they studied mostly in relation to multiple sclerosis and other myelin-destroying autoimmune diseases. As it turned out, researchers were mostly correct—neurons and synapses can indeed explain almost every class of mental phenomena: memory, emotion, muscle control, sensory perception, and so on. But there's a key question that neurons can't explain: why does it take people so long to learn complex skills?

One of the first clues to myelin's role was uncovered in the mid-1980s by an experiment involving rats and Tonka toy dump trucks. Bill Greenough at the University of Illinois raised three groups of rats in varying ways. In the first group individual rats were isolated from other rats, each one in a large plastic shoebox. The rats in the second group were raised with other rats but also in shoeboxes. The rats in the third group, however, were raised in an enriched environment, surrounded by other rats and a pile of toys that they instinctively played with, even to the point of figuring out how to work the lever on the dump truck.

When Greenough autopsied the animals' brains after two months, he found that the number of synapses in the enriched-environment group had increased by 25 percent compared with the other two groups. Greenough's work was well received, helping establish the idea of brain plasticity, in particular the notion that the brain has critical developmental windows, during which its growth responds to its environment. But buried in Greenough's study was a secondary finding that was largely ignored by the scientific community. Something else had also grown by 25 percent in the enriched-environment group: white matter—myelin.

"We'd been ignoring myelin; everybody thought it was a bystander," Greenough said. "But then it became clear that big things were happening there."

Still, neurons and synapses continued to get the lion's share of research attention until around 2000, when a powerful new technology called diffusion tensor imaging allowed neurologists to measure and map myelin inside living subjects. Suddenly researchers began to link structural deficiencies in myelin to a variety of disorders, including dyslexia, autism, attention deficit disorder, post-traumatic stress syndrome, and even pathological lying. While many researchers focused on myelin's link to disease, another group became interested in the role it might play in normal, even high-functioning, individuals.

More studies followed. In 2005 Fredrik Ullen scanned the brains of concert pianists and found a directly proportional relationship between hours of practice and white matter. In 2000 Torkel Klingberg linked reading skill to white matter increases, and in 2006 Jesus Pujol did the same for vocabulary development. In 2005 the Cincinnati Children's Hospital study of 47 normal children aged 5 to 18 correlated increased IQ with increased organization and density of white matter.

Other researchers, like Dr. Fields, uncovered the mechanism by which these myelin increases happened. As he described in a 2006 paper in the journal *Neuron,* supporter cells called oligodendrocytes and astrocytes sense the nerve firing and respond by wrapping more myelin on the fiber that fires. The more the nerve fires, the more myelin wraps around it. The more myelin wraps around it, the faster the signals travel, increasing velocities up to one hundred times over signals sent through an uninsulated fiber.

The studies piled up, gradually coalescing into a new picture. Myelin is infrastructure all right, but with a powerful twist: within the vast metropolis of the brain, myelin quietly transforms narrow alleys into broad, lightning-fast super-highways. Neural traffic that once trundled along at two miles an hour can, with myelin's help, accelerate to two hundred miles an hour. The refractory time (the wait required between one signal and the next) decreases by a factor of 30. The increased speed and decreased refractory time combine to boost overall information-processing capability by 3,000 times—broadband indeed.

What's more, myelin has the capacity to regulate velocity, speeding or occasionally even slowing signals so they hit synapses at the optimal time. Timing is vital because neurons are binary: either they fire or they don't, no gray area. Whether they fire depends solely on whether the incoming impulse is big enough to exceed their threshold of activation. To explain the implications, Fields had me imagine a skill circuit where two neurons have to combine their impulses to make a third high-threshold neuron fire—for, say, a golf swing. But here's the catch: in order to combine properly, those two incoming impulses must arrive at nearly exactly the same time—sort of like two small people running at a heavy door to push it open. That required time window turns out to be about 4 milliseconds, or about half the time it takes a bee to flap its wings once. If the first two signals arrive more than 4 milliseconds apart, the door stays shut, the crucial third neuron doesn't fire, and the golf ball soars into the rough. "Your brain has so many connections and possibilities that your genes can't code the neurons to time things so precisely," Fields said. "But you can build myelin to do it."

While the precise mechanism of optimization remains a mystery for now—Fields theorizes that a feedback loop is at work, monitoring, comparing, and integrating outputs—the overall picture adds up to a process elegant enough to please

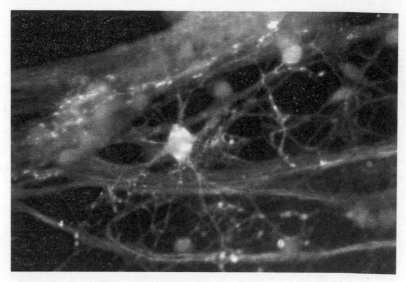

This is the learning moment, when the circuits fire and the oligos reach out and start wrapping the nerve fiber with myelin. This is skill being born. (From R. Douglas Fields, "White Matter Matters," *Scientific American* (2008), p. 46.

Darwin himself: nerve firings grow myelin, myelin controls impulse speed, and impulse speed is skill. Myelin doesn't make synapses unimportant—to the contrary, Fields and other neurologists emphasize that synaptical changes remain key to learning. But myelin plays a massive role in how that learning manifests itself. As Fields put it, "Signals have to travel at the right speed, arrive at the right time, and myelination is the brain's way of controlling that speed."

Myelin theory, as seen through the eyes of Dr. Fields, is impressive. But what stayed with me was what he showed me next: a glimpse into a deep-practicing brain. We walked down the narrow hall to a colleague's office and saw what looked like an undersea image out of Jules Verne: glowing green squidlike shapes against a field of black, their tentacles reaching for slender fibers. The squids, Fields informed me, are oligodendrocytes—oligos, in lab lingo, the cells that produce the myelin. When a nerve fiber fires, the oligo senses it, grabs hold, and starts wrapping. Each tentacle curls and extends as the oligo squeezes cytoplasm out of itself until only a cellophanelike sheet of myelin remains. That myelin, still attached to the oligo, proceeds to wrap over and over the nerve fiber with unworldly precision, spiraling down on each end to create the distinctive sausage shape, tightening itself like a threaded nut along the fiber.

"It's one of the most intricate and exquisite cell-to-cell processes there is," Fields said. "And it's slow. Each one of these wraps can go around the nerve fiber forty or fifty times, and that can take days or weeks. Imagine doing that to an entire neuron, then an entire circuit with thousands of nerves. It would be like insulating a transatlantic cable."*

So there's the picture in a nutshell: each time we deeply practice a nine-iron swing or a guitar chord or a chess opening, we are slowly installing broadband in our circuitry. We are firing a signal that those tiny green tentacles sense; they react by reaching toward the nerve fibers. They grasp, they squish, and they make another wrap, thickening the sheath. They build a little more insulation along the wire, which adds a bit more bandwidth and precision to the skill circuit, which translates into an infinitesimal bit more skill and speed. Struggle is not optional—it's neurologically required: in order to get your skill circuit to fire optimally, you must by definition fire the circuit suboptimally; you must make mistakes and pay

---

* A darker, more vivid way to appreciate myelin's role in skill development is to consider diseases that attack myelin. British cellist Jacqueline du Pré mysteriously lost her ability to perform at age twenty-eight and was diagnosed with multiple sclerosis eight months later. Such diseases are quite literally the opposite of acquiring skill, as they destroy myelin while leaving the connections between neurons mostly intact

attention to those mistakes; you must slowly teach your circuit. You must also keep firing that circuit—i.e., practicing—in order to keep myelin functioning properly. After all, myelin is living tissue.

To sum up: it's time to rewrite the maxim that practice makes perfect. The truth is, practice makes myelin, and myelin makes perfect. And myelin operates by a few fundamental principles.

1.   **The firing of the circuit is paramount.** Myelin is not built to respond to fond wishes or vague ideas or information that washes over us like a warm bath. The mechanism is built to respond to actions: the literal electrical impulses traveling down nerve fibers. It responds to urgent repetition. In a few chapters we'll discuss the likely evolutionary reasons, but for now we'll simply note that deep practice is assisted by the attainment of a primal state, one where we are attentive, hungry, and focused, even desperate.

2.   **Myelin is universal.** One size fits all skills. Our myelin doesn't "know" whether it's being used for playing shortstop or playing Schubert: regardless of its use, it grows according to the same rules. Myelin is meritocratic: circuits that fire get insulated. If you moved to China, your myelin would wrap fibers that help you conjugate Mandarin verbs. To put it another way, myelin doesn't care who you are—it cares what you do.

3.   **Myelin wraps—it doesn't unwrap.** Like a highway-paving machine, myelination happens in one direction. Once a skill circuit is insulated, you can't un-insulate it (except through age or disease). That's

why habits are hard to break. The only way to change them is to build new habits by repeating new behaviors—by myelinating new circuits.

4. **Age matters.** In children, myelin arrives in a series of waves, some of them determined by genes, some dependent on activity. The waves last into our thirties, creating critical periods during which time the brain is extraordinarily receptive to learning new skills. Thereafter we continue to experience a net gain of myelin until around the age of fifty, when the balance tips toward loss. We retain the ability to myelinate throughout life—thankfully, 5 percent of our oligos remain immature, always ready to answer the call. But anyone who has tried to learn a language or a musical instrument later in life can testify that it takes a lot more time and sweat to build the requisite circuitry. This is why the vast majority of world-class experts start young. Their genes do not change as they grow older, but their ability to build myelin does.

On one level, the study of myelin sounds like an exotic new neuroscience. But on another level, myelin is similar to another evolution-built mechanism you use every day: muscles. If you use your muscles a certain way—by trying hard to lift things you can barely lift—those muscles will respond by getting stronger. If you fire your skill circuits the right way—by trying hard to do things you can barely do, in deep practice—then your skill circuits will respond by getting faster and more fluent.

Views about our use of muscles have changed. Until the 1970s relatively few people ran marathons or pursued bodybuilding;

those who did and excelled were considered to possess a special gift. That worldview flipped when we learned how the human cardiovascular system actually works: that we can improve it by targeting our aerobic or anaerobic systems, that we can strengthen our heart and muscles by pushing ourselves to operate at the outer edges of our ability—lifting a slightly heavier weight, or trying to run a slightly farther distance. It turned out that regular people could become bodybuilders or marathoners gradually, by tapping into the power of the mechanism.

Thinking about skill as a muscle requires a big adjustment—you might say that we have to build a new circuit of understanding. For the last century and a half, we've understood talent through a Darwin-inspired model of genes and environment, a.k.a. nature and nurture. We've grown up belieing that genes impart unique gifts, and that environment offers unique opportunities for expressing those gifts. We've instinctively chalked up the kind of success we see in remote, impoverished hotbeds like Brazil's soccer fields to the vague notion that underdogs try harder and want it more. (Never mind that the world is brimming with millions of desperately poor people who try desperately hard to succeed at soccer.) But the myelin model shows that certain hotbeds succeed not only because people there are trying harder but also because they are trying harder in the right way—practicing more deeply and earning more skill. When we look more closely, those hotbeds aren't really underdogs at all. Like David, they have found the right leverage against Goliath.

ANDERS ERICSSON'S BIG ADVENTURE

Myelin science is still in its early days. As one neurologist told me, until a few years ago all the world's myelin researchers could have fit into a single restaurant. "When it comes to myelin, we know perhaps two percent of what we know about synapses," Fields said. "We're on the frontier."

This doesn't mean the scientists who are studying myelin fail to see its massive potential, or that the new model doesn't influence the way they see the world. (When Fields and I played pool at his house, he commented that he "hasn't myelinated his pool-playing circuits that much.") But it does mean that they harbor a deep yearning for a major, broad-based study to investigate myelin's relationship to human skill and learning.

This is no small wish. The ideal myelin study would be biblical in scope. It would examine all types of skill, in all conceivable environments. It would be a project worthy of Noah, requiring someone obsessed enough to track and measure each species of skill, then to metaphorically march a miles-long procession of ballplayers, artists, singers, chess players, and physicists into a single massive inquiry. To myelin researchers, now busily probing petri dishes, the notion of such a grand study is romantic, irresistible, and utterly outlandish. What kind of person—what kind of maniacally energetic Noah—would take on such a project?

This is where Anders Ericsson enters our story. Ericsson was born in 1947 in a northern suburb of Stockholm, Sweden. As a boy, Ericsson idolized famous explorers, in particular Sven Anders Hedin, Scandinavia's turn-of-the-century version of Indiana Jones. Hedin was an irresistible character: a supremely talented linguist, archaeologist, paleontologist, artist, and geographer who had explored the far reaches of Mongolia, Tibet, and the Himalayas, routinely cheating death and writing highly regarded books. From within the confines of his small suburban bedroom, Ericsson studied Hedin's works, envisioning his own worlds to discover and explore.

As he grew older, however, Ericsson's dreams encountered difficulties. Most of the world's frontiers appeared to have been explored, the blank spots on the map filled in. And unlike Hedin, Ericsson appeared to be mostly without talent. While he was decent at math, he was fairly hopeless at soccer and basketball, languages, biology, and music. When he was fifteen, Ericsson discovered he was good at chess, regularly winning lunchtime matches against his fellow students. It seemed he'd discovered his talent—for a few weeks. Then one of the boys—one of the worst players in the group, in fact—suddenly improved and started trouncing Ericsson every time. Ericsson was mad.

He was also curious. "I really thought about this a lot," he said. "What had just happened? Why could that boy, whom I had beaten so easily, now beat me just as easily? I knew he was studying, going to a chess club, but what had happened, really, underneath? From that point on I deliberately tried to avoid getting really good at something. I gradually became more obsessed with studying experts than with being one."

In the mid-1970s Ericsson was studying psychology at the Royal Institute of Technology. At the time the field of psychology was in an awkward state of transition, stretched between two divergent schools of thought: on one hand, Sigmund Freud and his ghostly closetful of unconscious urges; on the other, B. F. Skinner and a steely-eyed behaviorist movement that treated humans as little more than collections of mathematical inputs and outputs. But the world was changing. In universities in England and the States, a movement called the cognitive revolution was beginning. This new theory, founded by a diverse group of psychologists, artificial-intelligence experts, and neuroscientists, held that the human mind operated like a computer that had been designed by evolution, and that it obeyed certain universal rules. As fate would have it, Sweden itself was enjoying a golden age of success in art and sport: a skinny unknown named Björn Borg was winning Wimbledon, Ingmar Bergman ruled world cinema, Ingemar Stenmark dominated skiing, and ABBA was conquering pop music. In Ericsson's mind, all of these disparate data mingled, giving him what he'd been looking for: fresh territory to explore. What was talent? What made successful people different from the rest of us? Where does greatness come from?

"I was looking for an area that gave me freedom," Ericsson said. "I was interested in how people accomplish great things, and at the time, that was viewed as outside the normal scope of inquiry."

Ericsson wrote his 1976 dissertation on the usefulness of verbal reports—people's accounts of their own mental states—as a tool for understanding their performance. His work caught the attention of psychologist-economist Herbert Simon, a pioneer of the cognitive revolution who would shortly collect a Nobel Prize in economics for his work on decision-making. Simon recruited Ericsson to come to America, and by 1977 Ericsson was working alongside Simon at Carnegie Mellon University in Pittsburgh, investigating basic questions of human problem-solving.

Characteristically, Ericsson's first project was to explore one of psychology's most sacred tenets: the belief that short-term memory is an innate, fixed quality. A famed 1956 paper by psychologist George Miller, called "The Magical Number Seven, Plus or Minus Two," established the rule that human short-term memory was limited to seven pieces of independent information (and gave Bell Telephone reason to settle on seven-digit phone numbers). The limit was called "channel capacity," and the capacity was believed to be as fixed as height or shoe size.

Ericsson set out to test Miller's theory in the simplest possible way: by training student volunteers to increase their capacity for memorizing strings of digits, as a new digit arrived once per second. To the scientific establishment, Ericsson's experiment seemed eccentric if not downright nuts, the equivalent of attempting to train people to increase their shoe size. Short-term memory was hardware. Seven digits was the limit; it didn't change.

When one of Ericsson's student volunteers memorized an eighty-digit number, the scientific establishment wasn't sure what to think. When the second volunteer surpassed one hundred digits, Miller's number seven seemed to have been replaced by a magic of a different sort. "People were blown away," Ericsson remembered. "They couldn't believe that there wasn't a universal limit. But it was true."

Ericsson showed that the existing model of short-term memory was wrong. Memory wasn't like shoe size—it could be improved through training. And this was when Ericsson had an insight: a glimpse of an unexplored territory worthy of his hero Hedin. If short-term memory wasn't limited, then what was? Every skill was a form of memory. When a champion skier flew down a hill, she was using structures of memory, telling her muscles what to do and when. When a master cellist played, he too was using structures of memory. Why wouldn't they all be subject to the same sort of training effect?

"Traditional theory said that hardware was a limit," Ericsson said. "But if people are able to transform the mechanism that mediates performance by training, then we're in an entirely new space. This is a biological system, not a computer. It can construct itself."

So began Ericsson's thirty-year odyssey through the kingdom of talent. Ericsson explored all dimensions of skilled performance, studying nurses, gymnasts, violinists, and dart players; Scrabble players, typists, and S.W.A.T. officers. He did not measure their myelin. (He's a psychologist, not a neurologist, and besides, diffusion tensor imaging hadn't been invented yet.) Instead he studied the talent process from an equally vital angle: he measured practice. Specifically, he measured the time and characteristics of practice.

Along with his colleagues in this field, Ericsson established a remarkable foundation of work (documented in several books and most recently in the appropriately Bible-size *Cambridge Handbook of Expertise and Expert Performance*). Its central tenet is a Gibraltar-like statistic: every expert in every field is the result of around ten thousand hours of committed practice. Ericsson called this process "deliberate practice" and defined it as working on technique, seeking constant critical feedback, and focusing ruthlessly on shoring up weaknesses. (For practical purposes, we can consider "deliberate practice" and "deep practice" to be basically the same thing—though since he's a psychologist, Ericsson's term refers to the mental state, not to myelin. For the record, he is attracted to the idea. "I find the correlation [between myelin and skill] very interesting," he told me.)

Along with researchers like Herbert Simon and Bill Chase, Ericsson validated hallmarks like the Ten-Year Rule, an intriguing finding dating to 1899, which says that world-class expertise in every domain (violin, math, chess, and so on) requires roughly a decade of committed practice. (Even the astonishing chess prodigy Bobby Fischer put in nine hard years before achieving his grandmaster status at age seventeen). This rule is often used to determine the ideal start of training: for example, in tennis girls peak physically at seventeen, so they ought to start at seven; boys peak later, so nine is okay. But the Ten-Year, Ten-Thousand-Hour Rule has more universal implications. It implies that all skills are built using the same fundamental mechanism, and further that the mechanism involves physiological limits from which no one is exempt.

In most minds, Ericsson's work inspires a singular and instinctive objection: What about geniuses? What about young Mozart's famous ability to transcribe entire scores on a single hearing? What about savants who saunter up to a piano or a Rubik's Cube and are instantly, magically brilliant? Ericsson and his colleagues reply with cool, irrefutable stacks of numbers. In *Genius Explained*, Dr. Michael Howe of Exeter University estimates that Mozart, by his sixth birthday, had studied 3,500 hours of music with his instructor-father, a fact that places his musical memory in the realm of impressive but obtainable skill. Savants tend to excel within narrow domains that feature clear, logical rules (piano and math—as opposed to, say, improvisational comedy or fiction writing). Furthermore, savants typically accumulate massive amounts of prior exposure to those domains, through such means as listening to music in the home. The true expertise of these geniuses, the research suggests, resides in their ability to deep-practice obsessively, even when it doesn't necessarily look like they're practicing. As Ericsson succinctly put it, "There's no cell type that geniuses have that the rest of us don't." That's not to say that a minuscule percentage of people don't possess an innate, obsessive desire to improve—what psychologist Ellen Winner calls "the rage to master." But these sorts of self-driven deep practicers are rare and are blazingly self-evident. (A rule of thumb: if you have to ask whether your child possesses the rage to master, he doesn't.)

If we overlay Ericsson's research with the new myelin science, we get something approaching a universal theory of skill that can be summed up in a temptingly concise equation: *deep practice* × *10,000 hours* = *world-class skill*. But the truth is, life's more complicated than that. The truth is, it's better to use the information as a lens through which we can illuminate how the talent code works, to uncover hidden connections between distant worlds, to ask strange questions, like: what do the Brontë sisters have in common with skateboarders?

Chapter 3

The Brontës, the Z-Boys, and the Renaissance

Excellence is a habit.
—Aristotle

THE GIRLS FROM NOWHERE

In the vast river of narratives that make up Western culture, most stories about talent are strikingly similar. They go like this: without warning, in the midst of ordinary, everyday life, a Kid from Nowhere appears. The Kid possesses a mysterious natural gift for painting/math/baseball/physics, and through the power of that gift, he changes his life and the lives of those around him.*

* This narrative of the divinely inspired artist is so tightly woven into our culture that it's easy to forget that there was a time when it didn't exist. Prior to the Italian Renaissance, skill at painting and sculpting was regarded as a useful craft, equivalent to masonry or weaving. Then, however, a painter named Giorgio Vasari invented the idea of the Heroic Artist. For his 1550 book *Lives of the Artists,* he told the story of a wandering shepherd boy named Giotto who was discovered in a field drawing marvelous sketches with a sharpened piece of stone, and who went on to become the first great artist of the Renaissance. Never mind that the story is historically unsubstantiated, or that, more to myelin's point, Giotto also spent years apprenticing to the master painter

Of all the compelling stories of youthful talent, the story of the Brontë sisters is tough to beat. Its essential arc was established by Elizabeth Gaskell in her 1857 *Life of Charlotte Brontë*. It went like this: far off in the remote moors of Haworth, West Yorkshire, within a drafty parsonage ruled by their icy, tyrannical father, three motherless sisters named Charlotte, Emily, and Anne wrote marvelous books before dying at a young age. In Gaskell's telling, the Brontës' story was a tragic fable, and the most magical part was that the children produced several of the greatest works of English literature. *Jane Eyre, Wuthering Heights, Agnes Grey,* and *The Tenant of Wildfell Hall*. The proof of their divine gift, Gaskell wrote, was the series of tiny books the Brontës created as children, books that wove fantastical stories of imaginary kingdoms called Glasstown, Angria, and Gondal.

As Gaskell related, "I have had a curious packet confided to me, containing an immense amount of manuscript, in an inconceivably small space; tales, dramas, poems, romances, written principally by Charlotte, in a hand which is almost impossible to decipher without the aid of a magnifying glass . . . When she gives way to her powers of creation, her fancy and her language alike run riot, sometimes to the very borders of apparent delirium."

Tiny books, delirium, supernaturally gifted children—it's high-octane stuff. Gaskell's book established a sturdy template into which most subsequent Brontë biographies have faithfully slid, in part due to the scarcity of original documents. Gaskell's narrative has been employed for a film, a stage play, and a morality tale. There's just one problem with

Cimabue. Vasari's irresistible notion of the divinely inspired lowborn child (which, after all, is not without its useful resonances) made for a marvelously captivating story and has proved durable and adaptable to many other fields.

Gaskell's narrative: it isn't true. To put it more precisely, the real story of the Brontës is even better.

The real story of the Brontës was uncovered by Juliet Barker, an Oxford-trained historian who spent six years as curator of the Brontë Parsonage Museum in Haworth. Scouring sources locally as well as across Europe, Barker assembled a trove of material that had gone mostly unexamined. In 1994 she systematically demolished Gaskell's myth with a 1,003-page firehose of scholarship called *The Brontës*.

In Barker's work, a fresh picture comes into focus. The town of Haworth was not a remote outpost but a moderately busy crossroads of politics and commerce. The Brontë home was a far more stimulating place than Gaskell portrayed, replete with books, current magazines, and toys, overseen by a benign, tolerant father. But the myth Barker upends most completely is the assertion that the Brontës were natural-born novelists. The first little books weren't just amateurish—a given, since their authors were so young—they lacked any signs of incipient genius. Far from original creations, they were bald imitations of magazine articles and books of the day, in which the three sisters and their brother Branwell copied themes of exotic adventure and melodramatic romance, mimicking the voices of famous authors and cribbing characters wholesale.

Barker's work conclusively establishes two facts about the Brontës' little books. First, they wrote a great deal in a variety of forms—twenty-two little books averaging eighty pages each in one fifteen-month period—and second, their writing, while complicated and fantastical, wasn't very good.* As

---

* Here's an early sample: "an Immense and terreble monster his head touched the clouds was encircled with a red and fiery Halo his nostrils flashed forth flames and smo smoke and he was enveloped in dim misty and indefinable robe." And so on. Reading their

Barker put it, "Their slap-dash writing, appalling spelling, and non-existent punctuation well into their late teenage years is usually glossed over [by Brontë biographers], as is the frequent immaturity of thought and characterization. These elements in the juvenilia do not detract from the Brontës' achievement in producing such a volume of literature at so early an age, but they do extensively undermine the view that they were born novelists."

Deep practice and myelin give us a better way to look at the Brontës. The unskilled quality of their early writing isn't a contradiction of the literary heights they eventually achieved—it's a prerequisite to it. They became great writers not *in spite of* the fact that they started out immature and imitative but *because* they were willing to spend vast amounts of time and energy being immature and imitative, building myelin in the confined, safe space of their little books. Their childhood writings were collaborative deep practice, where they developed storytelling muscles. As Michael Howe wrote of the Brontës in *Genius Explained,* "The fact that the creative activity of writing about an invented world was a joint exercise contributed enormously to the authors' enjoyment. It was a marvelous game, in which each participant eagerly ingested and responded to their sibling's latest installment."

To write a book, even a tiny one, is to play a particular kind of game. Rules must be formed and obeyed. Characters must be conceived and constructed. Landscapes must be described. Lines of narrative must be puzzled out and followed. Each of these can be thought of as a distinct action, the firing of a circuit that's linked to other circuits. Written far from parental

---

little books makes you realize that, for the Brontës, the act of writing was profoundly social, sort of like playing Dungeons and Dragons. Except, of course, that the Brontës had the challenge and privilege of inventing the whole thing.

eyes, removed from any formal pressure, the little books functioned as the equivalent of a Link trainer, a place where the Brontë sisters fired and honed millions upon millions of circuits, tangled and untangled thousands of authorial knots, and created hundreds of works that were utter artistic failures except for two redeeming facts: each one made them happy, and each one quietly earned them a bit of skill. *Skill is insulation that wraps neural circuits and grows according to certain signals.*

When Emily Brontë's *Wuthering Heights* was published in 1847, reviewers marveled at the author's originality. Here was a complex masterpiece of imaginative storytelling, featuring the frightening, fascinating character of Heathcliff, a brooding outsider whose only redeeming characteristic was his love for free-spirited Catherine, who tragically marries the wealthy, refined Edgar Linton. Critics were right to marvel but wrong about the originality. In the scribbles of the little books, we can find all the elements waiting to be assembled: the misty poetic landscape (called Gondal), the dark hero (christened Julius Brenzaida), the headstrong heroine (Augusta Geraldine Almeda), and the rich suitor (Lord Alfred). Seen in this light, it's not surprising that Emily Brontë was able to write the story so well. After all, she had been deep-practicing it for quite some time.

The Myelin Skaters

In the mid-1970s the world of skateboarding was turned upside down by a small group of kids who called themselves the Z-Boys. A band of lanky, sun-bleached teenagers from a surf shop near Venice, California, the Z-Boys skated in a way no one had ever seen. They did aerial maneuvers. They scraped their boards along curbs and handrails. They carried themselves with a punk-outsider sensibility that we now recognize as the sport's lingua franca. Most usefully, they had a gift for dramatic timing, making their debut at the Bahne-Cadillac Skateboard Championship in Del Mar, California, in the summer of 1975. According to witnesses, the Z-Boys were mysterious outsiders, rawboned geniuses who had descended on the previously sedate sport with all the impact, if not the subtlety, of Genghis Khan. As the London *Guardian* summed up in its review of a documentary film on the Z-Boys: "[A]s [Jay] Adams slips into a loose crouch, grabs both ends of his board, and hops up and down in a burst of explosive energy speeding across the platform, the implication is clear already. In his charge, a skateboard is no longer a piece of sporting equipment, like a tennis racket. Instead, it's more like an electric guitar, an instrument for aggressive, irreverent, spontaneous self-expression."

But such expression was, in fact, far from spontaneous. Most of the Z-Boys were dedicated ocean surfers, having logged hundreds of hours on their boards. On days when the waves failed to show, they had simply transferred their aggressive, low-slung surfer style to the street. Another factor in their rise to greatness was more accidental: the discovery, in the early 1970s, of a unique tool, a myelin accelerant that allowed them to improve their circuitry at a ferocious speed. That tool was an empty swimming pool.

Thanks to a combination of drought, fire, and overbuilt real estate, the neighborhoods of Bel Air and Beverly Hills were rife with empty pools. Finding them was easy: the Z-Boys drove down side streets with a scout standing on the roof of their car, scanning over fences for likely venues. Riding the pool's steep curved walls was difficult at first. The first days brought some spectacular wipeouts (not to mention more than a few police calls from surprised homeowners). But sometime in 1975, in a moment that qualifies as skateboarding's version of the Wright brothers at Kitty Hawk, the Z-Boys achieved liftoff.

"When we hit the pools it became a really serious activity—the most serious activity," said Skip Engblom, part owner of the surf shop and the group's de facto mentor. "Every time we had to go bigger, faster, longer. We were like a painter with a new canvas."

In *Skateboard Kings,* a 1978 British documentary, a skater identified as Ken described the experience. "Pool riding is definitely the hardest thing to do," he said. "It takes whole-body coordination, so different than any other part of skateboarding... But like, when I'm doing it, I flash on certain things, like I'm coming up to the top, I hit the top, and I feel if it's a good connection or not, and that will either send me into a slide across the top, or else I go for air . . . You're just out there, and then you just want to make it, and you feel more air and more air and if you have it under control you just totally go for it."

Consider the pattern of actions that Ken describes. The space and shape of the pool constrain his efforts and narrow his focus to certain flashes, to certain connections that are either made or not made. It's fly high or fall hard: there are no gray areas, no mushiness. Once inside the pool, sliding along the steep surface, the Z-Boys had to play by the rules of the new game. From a deep-practice point of view, the empty swimming pool created a world not unlike that of the little books of the Brontë sisters or the futsal courts of Brazil. Circuits are fired and honed. Mistakes are made and corrected.

Myelin flourishes. Talent blooms. *Skill is insulation that wraps neural circuits and grows according to certain signals.*

For the last few hundred years, Western culture has understood and explained talent using the idea of unique identity— the tumble of cosmic dice that makes everyone different, and a few lucky people special. According to that way of thinking, the Brontës and the Z-Boys succeeded because they were exceptional—mysteriously gifted outsiders, destiny-kissed Kids from Nowhere. Seen through the lens of deep practice, however, the story flips. Uniqueness still matters, but its significance resides in the way the Brontës and the Z-Boys do the things necessary to build their remarkable skills: firing the right signals, honing circuits, making tiny books and filling them with childish stories, searching out empty swimming pools so that they can spend hours riding and falling inside them. The truth is, plenty of other Yorkshire girls had lives just as parochial and constricted as the Brontës', just as plenty of other Los Angeles kids were as edgy and cool as the Z-Boys. But myelin doesn't care about who you are. It only cares about what you do.

We've seen how deep practice and myelin illuminate the talents of small groups of people. Now let's apply those ideas to two slightly larger groups. First, we'll look at the artists of the Italian Renaissance. Then we'll look at a slightly bigger group: the human species.

THE MICHELANGELO SYSTEM

A few years ago a Carnegie Mellon University statistician named David Banks wrote a short paper entitled "The Problem of Excess Genius." Geniuses are not scattered uniformly through time and space, he pointed out; to the contrary, they tend to appear in clusters. "The most important question we can ask of historians is, 'Why are some periods and places so astonishingly more productive than the rest?'" Banks wrote. "It is intellectually embarrassing that this is almost never posed squarely ... although its answer would have thrilling implications for education, politics, science, and art."

Banks singled out three main clusters of greatness: Athens from 440 B.C. to 380 B.C., Florence from 1440 to 1490, and London from 1570 to 1640. Of these three none is so dazzling or well documented as Florence. In the space of a few generations a city with a population slightly less than that of present-day Stillwater, Oklahoma, produced the greatest outpouring of artistic achievement the world has ever known. A solitary genius is easy to understand, but dozens of them, in the space of two generations? How could it happen?

Banks listed the conventional-wisdom explanations for the Renaissance:

Prosperity, which provided money and markets to support art

Peace, which provided the stability to seek artistic and philosophical progress

Freedom, which liberated artists from state or religious control

Social mobility, which allowed talented poor people to enter the arts

The paradigm thing, which brought new perspectives and mediums that created a wave of originality and expression.

All of these seem to be likely causes, Banks wrote, and it is superficially plausible that by remarkable good fortune they converged to spark the Renaissance. Unfortunately, he continued, the actual existence of most of these factors is contradicted by the historical record. While socially mobile, Florence in the 1400s wasn't unusually prosperous, peaceful, or free. In fact, the city was recovering from a disastrous plague, was divided by vigorous fighting among powerful families, and was ruled by the church's iron fist.

So, the usual thinking goes, perhaps it's the reverse. Perhaps it's the infighting, plagues, and restrictive church that formed the convergence. And yet this logic too collapses under its own weight, since there are plenty of other places that had these factors present and yet did not produce anything resembling Florence's collection of great artistic talent.

Banks's paper neatly illustrates the endless cycle of tail-chasing that ensues when you apply traditional nature/nurture thinking to questions of talent. The more you try to distill the vast ocean of potential factors into a golden concentrate of uniqueness, the more contradictory the evidence becomes, and the more you are nudged toward the seemingly inescapable conclusion that geniuses are simply born and that phenomena like the Renaissance were thus a product of blind luck. As historian Paul Johnson writes, giving voice to that theory, "Genius suddenly comes to life and speaks out of a vacuum, and then it is silent, equally mysteriously."

Now let's look at the problem through the prism of deep practice. Myelin doesn't care about prosperity, peace, or paradigms. It doesn't care what the church was doing, or who died in the plague, or how much money anyone had in the bank. It asks the same questions we ask of the Brontës and the Z-Boys:

What did Florentine artists *do*? How did they practice, and for how long?

As it turns out, Florence was an epicenter for the rise of a powerful social invention called craft guilds. Guilds (the word means "gold") were associations of weavers, painters, goldsmiths, and the like who organized themselves to regulate competition and control quality. Guilds worked like employee-owned corporations. They had management, dues, and tight policies dictating who could work in the craft. What they did best, however, was grow talent. Guilds were built on the apprenticeship system, in which boys around seven years of age were sent to live with masters for fixed terms of five to ten years.

An apprentice worked directly under the tutelage and supervision of the master, who frequently assumed rights as the child's legal guardian. Apprentices learned the craft from the bottom up, not through lecture or theory but through action: mixing paint, preparing canvases, sharpening chisels. They cooperated and competed within a hierarchy, rising after some years to the status of journeyman and eventually, if they were skilled enough, master. This system created a chain of mentoring: da Vinci studied under Verrocchio, Verrocchio studied under Donatello, Donatello studied under Ghiberti; Michelangelo studied under Ghirlandaio, Ghirlandaio studied under Baldovinetti, and so on, all of them frequently visiting one another's studios in a cooperative-competitive arrangement that today would be called social networking.*

In short, apprentices spent thousands of hours solving problems, trying and failing and trying again, within the confines of a world built on the systematic production of excellence.

---

* The system lasted until the 1500s, when powerful new nation-states rose up to put an end to the guilds and with them the deep-practice engine of the Renaissance.

Their life was roughly akin to that of a twelve-year-old intern who spends a decade under the direct supervision of Steven Spielberg, painting sets, sketching storyboards, setting cameras. The notion that such a kid might one day become a great film director would hardly be a surprise: it would be closer to unavoidable (see Ron Howard).

Consider Michelangelo. From ages six to ten he lived with a stonecutter and his family, learning how to handle a hammer and chisel before he could read and write. After a brief, unhappy attempt at schooling, he apprenticed to the great Ghirlandaio. He worked on blockbuster commissions, sketching, copying, and preparing frescoes in one of Florence's largest churches. He was then taught by master sculptor Bertoldo and tutored by other luminaries at the home of Lorenzo de' Medici, where Michelangelo lived until he was seventeen. He was a promising but little-known artist until he produced the *Pietà* at age twenty-four. People called the *Pietà* pure genius, but its creator begged to differ. "If people knew how hard I had to work to gain my mastery," Michelangelo later said, "it would not seem so wonderful at all."

"The apprenticeship system, with its long period of study, early acquaintance with varied materials, copying, and collaborative work, somehow allowed boys who were probably quite ordinary in every respect to be turned into men possessing a high degree of artistic skill," wrote Bruce Cole in *The Renaissance Artist at Work*. "Art—so the Renaissance believed— could be taught by a series of progressive steps from grinding colors, to making copies, to work on the master's design, to inventing one's own paintings or sculptures."

We tend to think of the great Renaissance artists as a homogenous group, but the truth is that they were like any other randomly selected group of people. They came from rich and poor families alike; they had different personalities, different teachers, different motivations. But they had one thing in common: they all spent thousands of hours inside a deep-practice hothouse, firing and optimizing circuits, correcting errors, competing, and improving skills. They each took part in the greatest work of art anyone can construct: the architecture of their own talent.

MEET MR. MYELIN

George Bartzokis is a professor of neurology at UCLA. Most of the time Bartzokis, who's in his fifties, resembles the sober, distinguished researcher and teacher he is: shirt and tie, neatly combed hair, courtly manner. But when he talks about myelin, something within him quickens. He leans forward hungrily. His eyes gleam; he smiles hugely. He looks as if he might suddenly leap out of his chair. Bartzokis does not want to behave in this way, but he can't help it. Around UCLA, he is known as "Mr. Myelin."

"Why do teenagers make bad decisions?" he asks, not waiting for an answer "Because all the neurons are there, but they are not fully insulated. Until the whole circuit is insulated, that circuit, although capable, will not be instantly available to alter impulsive behavior as it's happening. Teens understand right and wrong, but it takes them time to figure it out.

"Why is wisdom most often found in older people? Because their circuits are fully insulated and instantly available to them; they can do very complicated processing on many levels, which is really what wisdom is. The volume of myelin in the brain continues to increase until around fifty, and you have to remember that it is alive: it is breaking down, and we are rebuilding it. Complex tasks like ruling countries or writing novels—these are most often better done by people who have built the most myelin.

"Why can't monkeys—which have every neuron type and neurotransmitter we have—use language the way we do?" he continues. "Because we've got twenty percent more myelin. To talk like we are now takes a lot of information-processing speed, and they have no broadband. Sure, you can teach a monkey to communicate at the level of a three-year-old, but beyond that, they are using the equivalent of copper wires."

Bartzokis keeps going, posing more questions, providing more answers, some documented, others awaiting the proof he knows will soon come.

- *Why do breast-fed babies have higher IQs?* Because the fatty acids in breast milk are the building blocks of myelin. This is why the FDA recently approved the addition of omega-3 fatty acids to infant formula, and also why eating fish, which is rich in fatty acids, has been linked to lowered risk of memory loss, dementia, and Alzheimer's disease. (Bartzokis takes DHA fatty acids daily.) The lesson in all cases is the same: the more myelin you have on board, the smarter you can be.

- *Why did Michael Jordan retire?* His muscles didn't change, but as with every other human being, his myelin started to break down with age—not much, but enough to prevent him from firing impulses at the speeds and frequencies required for Michael Jordan–esque explosive movement.

- *Why was puny Cro-Magnon man able to survive, when bigger, stronger, larger-brained Neanderthals died out?* Because Cro-Magnons had more myelin; they could outthink, outcommunicate, and ultimately outcompete the Neanderthals. (Bartzokis is awaiting DNA testing of a Neanderthal tooth that he says may confirm his hypothesis.)

- *Why can horses walk immediately on being born while humans take a year?* A horse is born with its muscles already myelinated, online, and ready to go. A baby's muscles, on the other hand, don't get myelinated for a year or so, and the circuits get optimized only with practice (see page 94 for more detail on this).

In selecting for myelin, "evolution made the same choice that any engineer designing the Internet would make," Bartzokis says. "It traded size of the computer for bandwidth. I don't care how big your computers are—what I want is to have them available instantaneously, so I can fully process things, *now*. That's what the Internet is, instant access to lots of computers. We operate by the same principles as Google does.

"We are myelin beings," Bartzokis says finally. "It's the way we're built. You can't avoid it."

We are myelin beings. This is a big statement. It offers a potentially revolutionary alternative to the traditional way we think about skill, talent, and human nature itself. To see what Mr. Myelin really means by it, however, we first must backtrack a moment.

Since Darwin, the traditional way of thinking about talent has gone something like this: genes (nature) and environment (nurture) combine to make us who we are.* In this view genes are the cosmic cards we are dealt, and the environment is the game in which they are played. Every once in a while fate produces a perfect combination of genes and environment, resulting in high levels of talent and/or genius.

Nature/nurture has been a terrifically popular model because it's clear and dramatic, and it speaks to a wide variety of phenomena in the natural world. But when it comes to explaining human talent, it has a slight problem: it's vague to the point of meaninglessness. Thinking that talent comes from genes and environment is like thinking that cookies come from sugar, flour, and butter. It's true enough, but not sufficiently detailed to be useful. To get beyond the outmoded nature/nurture model, we need to begin with a clear picture of how genes actually work.

Genes are not cosmic playing cards. They are evolution-tested instruction books that build the immensely complicated machines that are us. They contain the blueprints, literally written in nucleotides, to construct our minds and bodies in the smallest detail. The task of design and construction is hugely complex but essentially straightforward: the genes instruct the cells to make the eyelash like *this,* the toenail like *that.*

When it comes to behavior, however, genes are forced to deal with a unique design challenge. Human beings move around through a big, varied world. They encounter all sorts of dangers, opportunities, and novel experiences. Things happen quickly, which means that behavior—skills—need to change quickly. The challenge is, how do you write an instruction book for behavior? How do our genes, sitting quietly inside

* The phrase *nature versus nurture* was not originally Darwin's but that of Sir Francis Galton, his lesser-known cousin, who spent a good portion of his life energetically but futilely trying to prove that genius was heritable.

our cells, help us adapt to an ever-changing, ever-dangerous world?

To help address this problem, our genes have evolved to do a sensible thing: they contain instructions to build our circuitry with preset urges, proclivities, instincts. Genes construct our brains so that when we encounter certain stimuli— a tasty meal, rotting meat, a stalking tiger, or a potential mate—a factory-loaded neural program kicks into gear, using emotions to guide our behavior in a useful direction. We feel hunger when we smell a meal, disgust when we smell rotten meat, fear when we see a tiger, desire when we see a potential mate. Guided by these preset neural programs, we navigate toward a solution.

That strategy works well for creating behaviors to deal with rotten meat and potential mates. After all, writing instructions to build an urge-circuit is relatively simple: *if X, then Y*. But what about creating complex higher behaviors, like playing the saxophone or Scrabble? As we've seen, higher skills are made of million-neuron chains working together with exquisite millisecond timing. The question of acquiring higher skills is really a question of design strategy. What's the best strategy for writing instructions to build a machine that can learn immensely complicated skills?

One obvious design strategy would be for the genes to prewire for the skill. The genes would provide detailed step-by-step instructions to build the precise circuits needed to perform the desired skill: to play music, or juggle, or do calculus. When the right stimulus came along, all the prebuilt wiring would connect up and start firing away, and the talent would appear: Babe Ruth starts whacking homers, Beethoven starts composing symphonies. This design strategy would seem to make sense (after all, what could be more straightforward?), but in fact it has two big problems.

First, it's expensive, biologically speaking. Building those elaborate circuits takes resources and time, which have to come at the expense of some other design feature. Second, it's a gamble with fate. Prewiring to create a genius software programmer doesn't help if it's 1850; and prewiring for a genius blacksmith would be useless today. In the space of a generation, or a few hundred miles, certain higher skills flip from being crucial to being trivial and vice versa.

To put it simply, prewiring a million-wire circuit for a complex higher skill is a stupid and expensive bet for genes to make. Our genes, however, having survived the gauntlet of the past few million years, aren't in the business of making stupid and expensive bets. (Other genes might have been, but they're long gone by now, along with the lineages that carried them.)*

Now let's consider a different design strategy. Instead of prewiring for specific skills, what if the genes dealt with the skill issue by building millions of tiny broadband installers and distributing them throughout the circuits of the brain? The broadband installers wouldn't be particularly complicated—in fact, they'd all be identical, wrapping wires with insulation to make the circuits work faster and smoother. They would work according to a single rule: whatever circuits are fired most, and most urgently, are the ones where the installers will go. Skill circuits that are fired often will receive more broadband; skills

---

* That's not to say that prewiring for complex behavior doesn't exist—for instance, look at bees and their flower-locating dance, or the mating rituals of any number of animals. But prewiring for those behaviors makes good evolutionary sense: they are crucial to survival, while playing piano and hitting a golf ball are not. (Well, mostly.)

that are fired less often, with less urgency, will receive less broadband.

Such broadband installers would be useful if they were preset to work most vigorously during youth, when we're adapting to our environment. They'd be efficient if they worked outside of our consciousness, without cluttering up the limited window of everyday experience. (After all, from a natural-selection point of view, it doesn't matter if we *feel* ourselves gaining the crucial skill, only that we gain it—similar to the workings of, say, our immune system.) From our limited vantage point, the increased skill would feel exactly like a gift, as if we were expressing some natural-born quality. But it would not be a gift: the real gift would be the tiny broadband installers, busily insulating whatever circuits were being fired, whether for hunting, math, music, or sport. Like all useful adaptations, the broadband-installer system would quickly have become standard operating equipment among the entire species.

We are myelin beings. The broadband is myelin, and the installers are the green squidlike oligodendrocytes, sensing the signals we send and insulating the corresponding circuits. When we acquire higher skills, we are co-opting this ancient adaptive mechanism to our individual ends, an event made possible by the fact that our genes let us—or more accurately, they let our needs and our actions—determine what skills we grow. This system is flexible, responsive, and economical, because it gives all human beings the innate potential to earn skill where they need it. The proof lies in the talent hotbeds, in the ten thousand hours people spend deep-practicing their way to world-class expertise, even in the strained Clint Eastwood facial expressions they share. These similarities are not accidental; they are the logical expression of a shared evolutionary mechanism built to respond to certain kinds of signals. *Skill is insulation that wraps neural circuits and grows according to certain signals.*

This is not to say that every person on the planet has the potential to become an Einstein (whose autopsied brain was found to contain an unusual amount of you-know-what).* Nor does it mean that our genes don't matter—they do. The point, rather, is that although talent feels and looks predestined, in fact we have a good deal of control over what skills we develop, and we each have more potential than we might ever presume to guess. We are all born with the opportunity to become, as Mr. Myelin likes to put it, lords of our own Internet.

The trick is to figure out how to do that.

---

* In 1985 Dr. Marian Diamond found that the left inferior parietal lobe of Einstein's brain, though it had an average number of neurons, had significantly more glial cells, which produce and support myelin, than the average person's brain. At the time the finding was considered so meaningless as to be nearly comical. But now it makes perfect sense, bandwidth-wise.

Chapter 4

The Three Rules of Deep Practice

Try again. Fail again. Fail better.
—*Samuel Beckett*

ADRIAAN DE GROOT AND THE HSE

Any discussion about the skill-acquiring process must begin by addressing a curious phenomenon that I came to know as the Holy Shit Effect. This refers to the heady mix of disbelief, admiration, and envy (not necessarily in that order) we feel when talent suddenly appears out of nowhere. The HSE is not the feeling of hearing Pavarotti sing or watching Willie Mays swing—they're one in a billion; we can easily accept the fact that they're different from us. The HSE is the feeling of seeing talent bloom in people who we thought were just like us. It's the tingle of surprise you get when the goofy neighbor kid down the street is suddenly lead guitarist for a successful rock band, or when your own child shows an inexplicable knack for differential calculus. It's the feeling of, where did *that* come from?

Traveling to talent hotbeds, I became plenty familiar with the HSE. First I would see young, cuddly kids (just like my kids!) trundling along to their classes, toting their cute baseball bats and tiny violins, making clumsy, endearing attempts at skill. They were just as unimpressive as you would expect children of that age to be. Then as the youngest kids departed and older kids started showing up, I witnessed a series of quantum leaps in skill level. Spending a few days at a hotbed was like walking down the hallway of a museum exhibition on the rise of the dinosaur. As if passing a series of dioramas, I encountered increasingly evolved species: the Pre-Teens (who were pretty darn good), the Mid-Teens (wow), and finally the Older Teenagers, who were velociraptors (take cover). The speed of the progression was stunning: each successive group was unimaginably stronger, faster, and more ferociously talented than the previous. Watching the change was like seeing an adorable gecko lizard morph into a slavering *T. Rex:* you know the two are related in theory, but that knowledge doesn't stop you from saying holy shit.

The interesting thing about the HSE is that it operates in one direction. The observer is dumbstruck, amazed, and bewildered, while the talent's owner is unsurprised, even blasé. This trick-mirror quality is not merely a case of diverging impressions—of willful naïveté on the observer's part or undue modesty on the talent-holder's part. It is a consistent perceptual pattern at the core of the skill-acquiring process, and it raises an important question: What's the nature of this process that creates two such wildly divergent realities? How can these people, who seem just like us, suddenly become talented while barely cognizant of how talented they've become? For the answer, we turn to a failed math teacher named Adriaan Dingeman de Groot.

De Groot, who was born in 1914, was a Dutch psychologist who played chess in his spare time. He experienced his own version of the HSE when a handful of players from his chess club, people just like him in age, experience, and background, nevertheless were able to perform superhuman feats of chess mastery. These were the sort of *T. Rex* players who could casually destroy ten opponents at once, blindfolded. Like Anders Ericsson decades later, de Groot puzzled over his losses, which led him to ask what exactly made these guys so great. At the time the scientific wisdom on the issue was unquestioned. It held that the best players possessed photographic memories that they used to absorb information and plan strategies. Master players succeeded, the theory went, because they were endowed with the cognitive equivalent of cannons, while the rest of us made do with popguns. But de Groot didn't buy this theory; he wanted to find out more.

To investigate, he set up an experiment involving both master players and more ordinary ones. De Groot placed chess pieces into positions from a real game, gave the players a five-second glimpse of the board, and then tested their recall. The results were what one might expect. The master players recalled the pieces and arrangements four to five times better than the ordinary players did. (World-class players neared 100 percent recall.)

Then de Groot did something clever. Instead of using patterns from a real chess game, he set the chess pieces in a random arrangement and reran the test. Suddenly the masters' advantage vanished. They scored no better than lesser players; in one case, a master chess player did worse than a novice. The master players didn't have photographic memories; when the game stopped resembling chess, their skills evaporated.

De Groot went on to show that in the first test, the masters were not seeing individual chess pieces but recognizing patterns. Where novices saw a scattered alphabet of individual pieces, masters were grouping those "letters" into the chess equivalent of words, sentences, and paragraphs. When the pieces became random, the masters were lost—not because they suddenly became dumber but because their grouping strategy was suddenly useless. The HSE vanished. The difference between chess *T. Rexes* and ordinary players was not the difference between a cannon and a popgun. It was a difference of organization, the difference between someone who understood a language and someone who didn't. Or, to put it another way, the difference between an experienced baseball fan (who can take in a game with an ascertaining glance—runner on third, two out, bottom of the seventh inning) and the same fan at his first cricket match (who spends the game squinting baffledly). Skill consists of identifying important elements and grouping them into a meaningful framework. The name psychologists use for such organization is *chunking*.

To get a feel for how chunking works, try to memorize these two sentences.

We climbed Mount Everest on a Tuesday morning.
Gn inromya Dseut Anotser ev e Tnuomde bmilcew.

The two sentences contain the same characters, just like de Groot's chessboards, except in the second sentence the order of those letters is reversed. The reason you can understand, recall, and manipulate the first sentence is that, like the chess masters or baseball fans, you have spent many hours learning and practicing a cognitive game known as reading. You've learned letter shapes and practiced chunking letters from left to right into discrete entities with deeper meanings—words—

and you've learned how to group those into still bigger chunks—sentences—that you can handle, move around, understand, and remember.

The first sentence is easy to remember because it has only three main conceptual chunks: "We climbed" is a chunk, "Mount Everest" is a chunk, and "Tuesday morning" is a chunk. Those chunks are in turn composed of smaller chunks. The letters *W* and *e* are both chunks that you combine into another chunk called *We*. The pattern of four diagonal lines forms a still smaller chunk that you recognize as a *W*. And so on—each group of chunks nests neatly inside another group like so many sets of Russian dolls. Your skill at reading, at its essence, is the skill of packing and unpacking chunks—or to put it in myelin terms, of firing patterns of circuits—at lightning speed.

Chunking is a strange concept. The idea that skill—which is graceful, fluid, and seemingly effortless—should be created by the nested accumulation of small, discrete circuits seems counterintuitive, to say the least. But a massive body of scientific research shows that this is precisely the way skills are built—and not just for cognitive pursuits like chess. Physical acts are also built of chunks. When a gymnast learns a floor routine, he assembles it via a series of chunks, which in turn are made up of other chunks. He's grouped a series of muscle movements together in exactly the same way that you grouped a series of letters together to form *Everest*. The fluency happens when the gymnast repeats the movements often enough that he knows how to process those chunks as one big chunk, the same way that you processed the above sentence. When he fires his circuits to do a backflip, the gymnast doesn't have to think, *Okay, I'm going to push off with my legs, arch my back, tuck my head into my shoulders, and bring my hips around,* any more than you have to process each letter of *Tuesday*. He simply fires the backflip circuit that he's built and honed through deep practice.

When chunking has been done effectively, it creates a mirage that gives rise to the HSE. From below, top performers look incomprehensibly superior, as if they've leaped in a single bound across a huge chasm. Yet as de Groot showed, they aren't nearly so different from ordinary performers as they seem. What separates these two levels is not innate superpower but a slowly accrued act of construction and organization: the building of a scaffolding, bolt by bolt and circuit by circuit—or as Mr. Myelin might say, wrap by wrap.*

Rule One: Chunk It Up

We've seen how deep practice is all about constructing and insulating circuits. But practically speaking, what does that feel like? How do we know we're doing it?

Deep practice feels a bit like exploring a dark and unfamiliar room. You start slowly, you bump into furniture, stop, think, and start again. Slowly, and a little painfully, you explore the space over and over, attending to errors, extending your reach into the room a bit farther each time, building a mental map until you can move through it quickly and intuitively.

Most of us do a certain amount of this practicing reflexively.

---

* De Groot published his study in 1946 to zero acclaim. It was rediscovered twenty years later by Anders Ericsson's mentor, Nobel laureate Herbert Simon, who acknowledged de Groot as a pioneer of cognitive psychology and who in 1965 helped publish the work in English as *Thought and Choice in Chess*. De Groot went on to employ his findings in his own life, competing as a master chess player, publishing widely, and at age eighty-eight, recording a CD of classical piano improvisations.

The instinct to slow down and break skills into their compo- nents is universal. We heard it a billion times while we were growing up, from parents and coaches who echoed the old re- frain "Just take it one step at a time." But what I didn't under- stand until I visited the talent hotbeds was just how effective that simple, intuitive strategy could be. In the talent hotbeds I visited, the chunking takes place in three dimensions. First, the participants look at the task as a whole—as one big chunk, the megacircuit. Second, they divide it into its smallest possi- ble chunks. Third, they play with time, slowing the action down, then speeding it up, to learn its inner architecture. People in the hotbeds deep-practice the same way a good movie director approaches a scene—one instant panning back to show the landscape, the next zooming in to examine a bug crawling on a leaf in slo-mo. We'll look at each technique to see how it is deployed.

ABSORB THE WHOLE THING.
This means spending time staring at or listening to the desired skill—the song, the move, the swing—as a single coherent entity. People in the hotbeds stare and listen in this way quite a lot. It sounds rather Zen, but it basically amounts to absorbing a picture of the skill until you can imagine yourself doing it.

"We're prewired to imitate," Anders Ericsson says. "When you put yourself in the same situation as an outstanding per- son and attack a task that they took on, it has a big effect on your skill."

Imitation need not be conscious, and in fact it often isn't. In California I met an eight-year-old tennis player named Carolyn Xie, one of the top-ranked age-group players in the country. Xie had a typical tennis prodigy's game, except for one thing. Instead of the usual two-handed backhand for that age, she hit one-handed backhands exactly like Roger Federer. Not a little bit like Federer but exactly like Federer, with that signature head-down, torero finish.

I asked Xie how she learned to hit that way. "I dunno," she said. "I just do." I asked her coach: he didn't know. Later Li Ping, Carolyn's mother, was chatting about their evening plans when she mentioned they'd be watching a tape of Roger's match. It turned out that everyone in the family was a huge fan of Federer; in fact, they had watched just about every televised match he'd ever played on tape. Carolyn in particular watched them whenever she could. In other words, in her short life she had seen Roger Federer hit a backhand tens of thousands of times. She had watched the backhand and, without knowing, simply absorbed the essence of it.*

Another example is Ray LaMontagne, a shoe-factory worker from Lewiston, Maine, who at age twenty-two had an epiphany that he should become a singer-songwriter. LaMontagne had little musical experience and less money, so he took a simple approach to learning: he bought dozens of used albums by Stephen Stills, Otis Redding, Al Green, Etta James, and Ray Charles, and holed up in his apartment. For two years. Every day he spent hours training himself by singing along to the records. LaMontagne's friends assumed he had left town; his neighbors assumed he was either insane or had locked himself inside a musical time capsule—which, in a sense, he had. "I would sing and sing, and hurt and hurt, because I knew I wasn't doing it right," LaMontagne said. "It

---

* W. Timothy Gallwey tells of a good example of imitation in his book *The Inner Game of Tennis*. When Gallwey was first teaching tennis in the 1960s, he decided to try an experiment: instead of talking to his beginner students, he would not speak a word, but simply show them how to hit. It worked surprisingly well, to the point that Gallwey was soon teaching fifty-year-old beginners to play passable games of tennis within twenty minutes without a single technical instruction.

took a long time, but I finally learned to sing from the gut." Eight years after he started, LaMontagne's first album sold nearly half a million copies. The main reason was his soulful voice, which *Rolling Stone* said sounded like church, and which other listeners mistook for that of Otis Redding and Al Green. LaMontagne's voice was a gift, it was agreed. But the real gift, perhaps, was the practice strategy he used to build that voice.

Some of the most fruitful imitation I saw took place at Spartak Tennis Club in Moscow, a freezing junkpile that has produced a volcano of talent: Anna Kournikova, Marat Safin, Anastasia Myskina, Elena Dementieva, Dinara Safina, Mikhail Youzhny, and Dmitry Tursunov. All in all, the club produced more top-twenty-ranked women than the United States did from 2005 to 2007, as well as half of the men's team that won the 2006 Davis Cup, and it's done all that with one indoor court. When I visited in December 2006, the club resembled a set for a *Mad Max* movie: shotgun shacks, diesel-shimmering puddles, and a surrounding forest filled with large, hungry, and disconcertingly speedy dogs. An abandoned eighteen-wheeler was parked out front. Walking up, I could see shapes moving behind clouded plastic windows, but I didn't hear that distinctive thwacking of tennis racquets and balls. When I walked in, the reason became evident: they were swinging all right. But they weren't using balls.

At Spartak it's called *imitatsiya*—rallying in slow motion with an imaginary ball. All Spartak's players do it, from the five-year-olds to the pros. Their coach, a twinkly, weathered seventy-seven-year-old woman named Larisa Preobrazhen-skaya, roamed the court like a garage mechanic tuning an oversize engine. She grasped arms and piloted small limbs slowly through the stroke. When they finally hit balls—one by one, in a line (there are no private lessons at Spartak),

Preobrazhenskaya frequently stopped them in their tracks and had them go through the motion again slowly, then once more. And again. And perhaps one more time.

It looked like a ballet class: a choreography of slow, simple, precise motions with an emphasis on *tekhnika*—technique. Preobrazhenskaya enforced this approach with an iron decree: none of her students was permitted to play in a tournament for the first three years of their study. It's a notion that I don't imagine would fly with American parents, but none of the Russian parents questioned it for a second. "Technique is *everything*," Preobrazhenskaya told me later, smacking a table with Khrushchev-like emphasis, causing me to jump and speedily reconsider my twinkly-grandma impression of her. "If you begin playing without technique, it is big mistake. Big, big mistake!"

BREAK IT INTO CHUNKS.

The place I visited that best displayed this process was the Meadowmount School of Music in upstate New York. Meadowmount is located a five-hour drive north of Manhattan in the green quilt of the Adirondack Mountains. Its founder, renowned violin teacher Ivan Galamian, chose this site for the same reason New York State builds most of its prisons in this area: it's remote, inexpensive, and extremely quiet. (Galamian had first settled the camp in nearby Elizabethtown but deemed the local girls to be too distractingly beautiful, a point he underlined by marrying one.)

The original camp comprised a few cabins and an old house that had no electricity, no running water, and no television or telephone service. Since then, little has changed. The grounds, while lovely, are basic: students sleep in spartan dorms, and individual practice cabins teeter on supports made of tree stumps, cinderblocks, and in several cases a jack taken from a nearby car. Meadowmount, however, is better defined by the camp's storied alumni (Yo-Yo Ma, Pinchas Zuckerman, Joshua Bell, and Itzhak Perlman) and, at its core, by a simple equation that has become the school's de facto motto: in seven weeks, most students will learn a year's worth of material, an increase of about 500 percent in learning speed. Among the students, this acceleration is well known but only dimly understood. So it's often spoken about as if it were some kind of snowboarding trick.

"Oh my God, that girl is totally gnarly," said David Ramos, sixteen, as he pointed out Tina Chen, a Chinese student who had recently performed a Korngold violin concerto at one of Meadowmount's nightly concerts. Ramos's voice dropped to an incredulous whisper. "She said she learned it in three weeks—but somebody else told me she really did it in *two*."

These feats are routine at Meadowmount, in part because the teachers take the idea of chunking to its extreme. Students scissor each measure of their sheet music into horizontal strips, which are stuffed into envelopes and pulled out in random order. They go on to break those strips into smaller fragments by altering rhythms. For instance, they will play a difficult passage in dotted rhythm (the horses' hooves sound—*da-dum, da-dum*). This technique forces the player to quickly link two of the notes in a series, then grants them a beat of rest before the next two-note link. The goal is always the same: to break a skill into its component pieces (circuits), memorize those pieces individually, then link them together in progressively larger groupings (new, interconnected circuits).

SLOW IT DOWN.

At Meadowmount jagged bursts of notes are stretched into whale sounds. One teacher has a rule of thumb: if a passerby can recognize the song being played, it's not being practiced correctly. When camp director Owen Carman teaches a class, he spends three hours covering a single page of music. New students are surprised at the seemingly glacial pace—it's three or five times slower than they've ever gone. But when they're finished, they have learned to play the page perfectly; such a Clarissa-like feat would otherwise take them a week or two of shallower practice.*

Why does slowing down work so well? The myelin model offers two reasons. First, going slow allows you to attend more closely to errors, creating a higher degree of precision with each firing—and when it comes to growing myelin, precision is everything. As football coach Tom Martinez likes to say, "It's not how fast you can do it. It's how slow you can do it correctly." Second, going slow helps the practicer to develop something even more important: a working perception of the skill's internal blueprints—the shape and rhythm of the interlocking skill circuits.

For most of the last century, many educational psychologists believed that the learning process was governed by fixed factors like IQ and developmental stages. Barry Zimmerman, a professor of psychology at City University of New York, has never been one of them. Instead, he's fascinated by the kind of learning that goes on when people observe, judge, and strategize their own performance—when they, in essence, coach themselves. Zimmerman's interest in this type of learning, known as *self-regulation*, led him in 2001 to undertake an experiment that sounds more like a street-magic stunt than

---

* A nice description of this effect, and of deep practice in general, comes from Abraham Lincoln's portrayal of his own learning process. "I am slow to learn and slow to forget what I have learned," Lincoln wrote. "My mind is like a piece of steel, very hard to scratch anything on it and almost impossible after you get it there to rub it out."

regular science. Working with Anastasia Kitsantas of George Mason University, Zimmerman posed a question: Is it possible to judge ability solely by the way people describe the way they practice? To take, for instance, a roomful of ballerinas of varying ability, query them about demi-pliés, and then accurately pick out the best dancer, second-best dancer, third-best dancer, and so on, based not on their performance but solely on how they talked about practicing those demi-pliés?

The skill Zimmerman and Kitsantas chose was a volleyball serve. They gathered a range of expert players, club players, and novices, and asked them how they approached the serve: their goals, planning, strategy choices, self-monitoring, and adaptation—twelve measures in all. Using the answers, they predicted the players' relative skill levels, then had the players execute their serve to test the accuracy of their predictions. The result? Ninety percent of the variation in skill could be accounted for by the players' answers.

"Our predictions were extremely accurate," Zimmerman said. "This showed that experts practice differently and far more strategically. When they fail, they don't blame it on luck or themselves. They have a strategy they can fix."

In other words, the volleyball experts are like de Groot's *T. Rex* chess players. Through practice, they had developed something more important than mere skill; they'd grown a detailed conceptual understanding that allowed them to control and adapt their performance, to fix problems, and to customize their circuits to new situations. They were thinking in chunks and had built those chunks into a private language of skill.

When I was at Meadowmount, I met a fourteen-year-old cellist named John Henry Crawford, who gave me one of the most useful descriptions of what deep practice feels like that I have heard. He was hanging out by himself in a decrepit garage that held one of Meadowmount's few concessions to leisure: a broken-down Ping-Pong table. Crawford talked about the feeling of acceleration he got at Meadowmount, which he called "clicking in."

"Last year it took me almost the whole seven weeks to click in and start practicing well," he said. "This year I can feel it happening already. It's a thought thing."

We started rallying; John Henry spoke with the rhythm of the ball.

"When I click in, every note is being played for a purpose. It feels like I'm building a house. It feels like, this brick goes here, that one goes there, I connect them and get a foundation. Then I add the walls, connect those. Then the roof, then the paint. Then, hopefully, it all hangs together."

We played a game. It was close for a while, then I went ahead 20–17. Then John Henry hit five straight killshots to win.

"What can I say?" He shrugged apologetically. "I guess I'm getting good at building this house too."

Rule Two: Repeat It

We're all familiar with the adage that practice is the best teacher. Myelin casts the truth of this old saying in a new light. There is, biologically speaking, no substitute for attentive repetition. Nothing you can do—talking, thinking, reading, imagining—is more effective in building skill than executing the action, firing the impulse down the nerve fiber, fixing errors, honing the circuit.

One way to illustrate this truth is through a riddle: What's the simplest way to diminish the skills of a superstar talent (short of inflicting an injury)? What would be the surest method of ensuring that LeBron James started clanking jump shots, or that Yo-Yo Ma started fudging chords?

The answer: don't let them practice for a month. Causing skill to evaporate doesn't require chromosomal rejiggering or black-ops psychological maneuvers. It only requires that you stop a skilled person from systematically firing his or her circuit for a mere thirty days. Their muscles won't have changed; their much-vaunted genes and character will remain unaltered; but you will have touched their talent at the weakest spot in its armor. Myelin, as Bartzokis reminds us, is living tissue. Like everything else in the body, it's in a constant cycle of breakdown and repair. That's why daily practice matters, particularly as we get older. As Vladimir Horowitz, the virtuoso pianist who kept performing into his eighties, put it, "If I skip practice for one day, I notice. If I skip practice for two days, my wife notices. If I skip for three days, the world notices."

Repetition is invaluable and irreplaceable. There are, however, a few caveats. With conventional practice, more is always better: hitting two hundred forehands a day is presumed to be twice as good as hitting one hundred forehands a day. Deep practice, however, doesn't obey the same math. Spending more time is effective—but only if you're still in the sweet spot at the edge of your capabilities, attentively building and honing circuits. What's more, there seems to be a universal limit for how much deep practice human beings can do in a day. Ericsson's research shows that most world-class experts—including pianists, chess players, novelists, and athletes—practice between three and five hours a day, no matter what skill they pursue.

People at most of the hotbeds I visited practiced less than

three hours a day. The younger Spartak kids (ages six to eight) practiced a mere three to five hours each week, while older teens ratcheted up to fifteen hours a week. The Little League baseballers of Curaçao, some of the world's best, play only seven months a year, usually three times a week. There were some exceptions—Meadowmount, for instance, insists on five hours of daily practice for its seven-week course. But on the whole the duration and frequency of practice in hotbeds seemed reasonably sane, proving what I saw in Clarissa's practices of "Golden Wedding" and "The Blue Danube": when you depart the deep-practice zone, you might as well quit.*

This jibes with what tennis coach Robert Lansdorp has witnessed. Lansdorp, who's in his sixties, is to tennis coaching what Warren Buffett is to investing, having worked with Tracy Austin, Pete Sampras, Lindsay Davenport, and Maria Sharapova. He is amused by the need of today's tennis stars to hit thousands of groundstrokes every day.

"You ever watch Connors practice? You ever watch McEnroe or Federer?" Lansdorp asks. "They didn't hit a thousand; most of them barely practice for an hour. Once you get timing, it doesn't go away."

Intrigued, I excitedly started to explain to Lansdorp about myelin—how it insulates circuits, how it grows slowly when we fire those circuits, how it takes ten years to get to world-class. I got about twenty seconds into my explanation when Lansdorp cut me off.

"Sure, of course," he said, nodding with the lordly style of someone who knows myelin more intimately than a neurologist ever could. "It has to be something like that."

*Another sign that the teachers look for is snoring. Deep practice tends to leave people exhausted: they can't maintain it for more than an hour or two at a sitting (a finding Ericsson has observed across many disciplines).

RULE THREE: LEARN TO FEEL IT

The summer I visited Meadowmount they offered a new course called "How to Practice," taught by Skye Carman, the sister of school director Owen Carman. Half a dozen teens filed into a small practice cabin. Skye, an ebullient personality and former concertmaster of the Holland Symphony, began by asking, "How many of you practice five or more hours a day?"

Four raised their hands.

Skye shook her head in disbelief. "Good for you. I could have never done that, not in a million billion years. See, I hate to practice! *Hate, hate, hate!* So what I did, I forced myself to make it as productive as it could be. So here's what I want to know. What's the first thing you do when you practice?"

They stared at her incomprehendingly.

"Tune. Play some Bach," a tall boy said finally. "I guess."

"Hmmmm," Skye said, raising her eyebrow, illuminating their lack of strategy. "Let me see. I'll bet you all just . . . play! I'll bet you tune, pick a piece you like, and start fooling with it. Like picking up a ball."

They nodded. She had them nailed.

"That's crazy!" she said, flinging her arms in the air. "Do you think athletes do that? Do you think they just fool around? You guys have to realize this is top sport. You *are* athletes. Your playing field is a few inches long, but it still is your field. You need to find a place to stand, know where you are. First, tune your instrument. *Then* tune your ear."

The point, Skye explained, is to get a balance point where you can sense the errors when they come. To avoid the mistakes, first you have to feel them immediately.

"If you hear a string out of tune, it should *bother* you,"

Skye told them. "It should bother you a *lot*. That's what you need to feel. What you're really practicing is concentration. It's a feeling. So now we're going to practice that feeling."

They closed their eyes, and she played an open string. Then she twisted a tuning peg a fraction of a millimeter, and the sound changed. Their smooth brows wrinkled, and their expressions turned irritated, faintly hungry for her to fix it. Skye smiled.

"There," she said quietly. "Remember that."

Myelin is sneaky stuff. It's not possible to sense myelin growing along your nerve fibers any more than you can sense your heart and lungs becoming more efficient after a workout. It is possible, however, to sense the telltale set of secondary feelings associated with acquiring new skills—the myelin version of "feeling the burn."

As I traveled to various talent hotbeds, I asked people for words that described the sensations of their most productive practice. Here's what they said:

Attention

Connect

Build

Whole

Alert

Focus

Mistake

Repeat

Tiring

Edge

Awake*

This is a distinctive list. It evokes a feeling of reaching, falling short, and reaching again. It's the language of mountain climbers, describing a sensation that is stepwise, incremental, connective. It's the feeling of straining toward a target and falling just short, what Martha Graham called "divine dissatisfaction." It's the feeling Glenn Kurtz writes about in his book *Practicing*: "Each day, with every note, practicing is the same task, this essential human gesture—reaching out for an idea, for the grandeur of what you desire, and feeling it slip through your fingers."

It's a feeling that brings to mind Robert Bjork's idea of the sweet spot: that productive, uncomfortable terrain located just beyond our current abilities, where our reach exceeds our grasp. Deep practice is not simply about struggling; it's about seeking out a particular struggle, which involves a cycle of distinct actions.

1. Pick a target.
2. Reach for it.
3. Evaluate the gap between the target and the reach.
4. Return to step one.

---

* Here is a list of words I didn't hear: *natural, effortless, routine, automatic*. Another word that's not used around the talent hotbeds I visited was *genius*. Not that geniuses don't exist: the teachers I spoke with pegged the genius rate at about one per decade. "Very occasionally we'll get a super-top genius talent. I have no idea how their brains function," said Meadowmount's Skye Carman. "But it's a tiny, tiny percentage. The rest of us mortals have to work at it."

Judging by the facial expressions I saw in talent hotbeds, the sweet spot might better be named the bittersweet spot. And yet that taste, like all others, can be acquired. One of the useful features of myelin is that it permits any circuit to be insulated, even those of experiences we might not enjoy at first. At Meadowmount, instructors routinely see students develop a taste for deep practice. They don't like it at first. But soon, they say, the students begin to tolerate and even enjoy the experience.

"Most kids accelerate their practice fairly quickly," said Meadowmount director Owen Carman. "I think of it as a turn inward; they stop looking outside for solutions and they reach within. They come to terms with what works and what doesn't. You can't fake it, you can't borrow, steal, or buy it. It's an honest profession."

Meadowmount teachers hawkeye the students for telltale signs: hieroglyphs of notes scribbled on the sheet music, a new intensity to the conversations, a fresh reverence for the warm-up routines. Sally Thomas, a violin teacher, watches for changes in the way they walk. "They show up here with a strut," Thomas said. "Then after a while they aren't strutting anymore. That's a good thing."

A larger-scale example of this phenomenon occurs in Japanese schools. According to a 1995 study, a sample of Japanese eighth graders spent 44 percent of their class time inventing, thinking, and actively struggling with underlying concepts. The study's sample of American students, on the other hand, spent less than 1 percent of their time in that state. "The Japanese want their kids to struggle," said Jim Stigler, the UCLA professor who oversaw the study and who cowrote *The Teaching Gap* with James Hiebert. "Sometimes the [Japanese] teacher will purposely give the wrong answer so the kids can grapple with the theory. American teachers, though, worked like waiters. Whenever there was a struggle, they wanted to move past it, make sure the class kept gliding along. But you don't learn by gliding."

Of all the images that communicate the sensation of deep practice, my favorite is that of the staggering babies. Long story short: a few years ago a group of American and Norwegian researchers did a study to see what made babies improve at walking. They discovered that the key factor wasn't height or weight or age or brain development or any other innate trait but rather (surprise!) the amount of time they spent firing their circuits, trying to walk.

However well this finding might support our thesis, its real use is to paint a vivid picture of what deep practice feels like. It's the feeling, in short, of being a staggering baby, of intently, clumsily lurching toward a goal and toppling over. It's a wobbly, discomfiting sensation that any sensible person would instinctively seek to avoid. Yet the longer the babies remained in that state—the more willing they were to endure it, and to permit themselves to fail—the more myelin they built, and the more skill they earned. The staggering babies embody the deepest truth about deep practice: to get good, it's helpful to be willing, or even enthusiastic, about being bad. Baby steps are the royal road to skill.

2

Ignition

Chapter 5

Primal Cues

*Every great and commanding moment in the annals
of the world is a triumph of some enthusiasm.*
—*Ralph Waldo Emerson*

"IF SHE CAN DO IT, WHY CAN'T I?"

Growing skill, as we've seen, requires deep practice. But deep practice isn't a piece of cake: it requires energy, passion, and commitment. In a word, it requires motivational fuel, the second element of the talent code. In this section we'll see how motivation is created and sustained through a process I call ignition. Ignition and deep practice work together to produce skill in exactly the same way that a gas tank combines with an engine to produce velocity in an automobile. Ignition supplies the energy, while deep practice translates that energy over time into forward progress, a.k.a. wraps of myelin.

When I visited the talent hotbeds, I saw a lot of passion. It showed in the way people carried their violins, cradled their soccer balls, and sharpened their pencils. It showed in the way they treated bare-bones practice areas as if they were cathedrals; in the alert, respectful gazes that followed a coach. The feeling wasn't always shiny and happy—sometimes it was dark and obsessive, and sometimes it was like the quiet, abiding love you see in old married couples. But the passion was always there, providing the emotional rocket fuel that kept them firing their circuits, honing skills, getting better.

When I asked people in the hotbeds about the source of their passion for violin/singing/soccer/math, the question struck most of them as faintly ridiculous, as if I were inquiring when they first learned to enjoy oxygen. The universal response was to shrug and say something like "I dunno, I've just always felt this way."

Faced with these responses, it's tempting to return the shrug, to chalk up their burning motivation to the unknown depths of the human heart. But this would not be accurate. Because in many cases it is possible to pinpoint the instant that passion ignited.

For South Korea's golfers, it was the afternoon of May 18, 1998, when a twenty-year-old named Se Ri Pak won the McDonald's LPGA Championship and became a national icon. (As one Seoul newspaper put it, "Se Ri Pak is not the female Tiger Woods; Tiger Woods is the male Se Ri Pak.") Before her, no South Korean had succeeded in golf. Flash-forward to ten years later, and Pak's countrywomen had essentially colonized the LPGA Tour, with forty-five players who collectively won about one-third of the events.

For Russia's tennis players, the moment came later that same summer when seventeen-year-old Anna Kournikova reached the Wimbledon semifinals and, thanks to her supermodel looks, gained the status of the world's most downloaded athlete. By 2004 Russian women were showing up regularly in major finals; by 2007 they occupied five of the top ten rankings and twelve of the top fifty. "They're like the goddamned Russian Army," said Nick Bollettieri, founder of his eponymous tennis academy in Bradenton, Florida. "They just keep on coming."

Year	South Koreans on LPGA Tour	Russians in WTA Top 100
1998	1	3
1999	2	5
2000	5	6
2001	5	8
2002	8	10
2003	12	11
2004	16	12
2005	24	15
2006	25	16
2007	33	15

Other hotbeds follow the same pattern: a breakthrough success is followed by a massive bloom of talent. Note that in each case the bloom grew relatively slowly at first, requiring five or six years to reach a dozen players. This is not because the inspiration was weaker at the start and got progressively stronger, but for a more fundamental reason: deep practice takes time (ten thousand hours, as the refrain goes). Talent is spreading through this group in the same pattern that dandelions spread through suburban yards. One puff, given time, brings many flowers.*

A different example of this phenomenon began on a blustery day in May 1954, when a skinny Oxford medical student named Roger Bannister became the first person to run a mile in less than four minutes. The broad outlines of his achievement are well known: how physiologists and athletes alike regarded the four-minute mile as an unbreakable physiological barrier; how Bannister systematically attacked the record; how he broke the mark by a fraction of a second, earning headlines around the world and lasting fame for what *Sports Illustrated* later called the single greatest athletic accomplishment of the twentieth century.

Less well known is what happened in the weeks after Bannister's feat: another runner, an Australian named John Landy, also broke the four-minute barrier. The next season a few more runners did too. Then they started breaking it in

---

* One of the useful things about this breakthrough-then-bloom pattern is that it makes it possible to forecast the rise of future talent hotbeds. I predict that one of them will be Venezuelan classical musicians. Gustavo Dudamel, a.k.a. El Dude, is the twenty-six-year-old wunderkind who now directs the Los Angeles Philharmonic. Most stories about him mention his off-the-chart skills, his signature curly hair, his charm. They don't mention the fact that Venezuela is producing lots of El Dudes through a program called the Fundación del Estado para el Sistema Nacional de las Orquestas Juveniles e Infantiles de Venezuela, known by its handier nickname of El Sistema (the system). The program enrolls poor kids into classical-training programs (250,000 kids at last count), brings the best players back as teachers, sends orchestras all over the world, and in general is starting to bear a striking resemblance to Venezuela's equally successful baseball academies. Another future hotbed will be Chinese novelists. Ha Jin (*Waiting*) looks to be the breakthrough performer of what might be a rather large contingent, including Ma Jian, Li Yiyun, Fan Wu, and Dai Sijie, which should arrive around the same time as the Chinese basketballers ignited by Yao Ming. Lastly, moviegoers should brace themselves for a wave of Romanian filmmakers, an unlikely group sparked by the four major prizes won at the Cannes Film Festival by that nation's directors over the last three years, as well as by the famously rigorous teaching at the Bucharest National University of Drama and Film.

droves. Within three years no fewer than seventeen runners
had matched the greatest sporting accomplishment of the
twentieth century. Nothing profound had changed. The track
surfaces were the same, the training was the same, the genes
were the same. To chalk it up to self-belief or positive thinking is to miss the point. The change didn't come from inside
the athletes: they were responding to something outside them.
The seventeen runners had received a clear signal—*you can
do this too*—and the four-minute mark, once an insurmount-
able wall, was instantly recast as a stepping-stone.

This is how ignition works. Where deep practice is a cool,
conscious act, ignition is a hot, mysterious burst, an awakening.
Where deep practice is an incremental wrapping, ignition works
through lightning flashes of image and emotion, evolution-
built neural programs that tap into the mind's vast reserves
of energy and attention. Where deep practice is all about
staggering-baby steps, ignition is about the set of signals and
subconscious forces that create our identity; the moments that
lead us to say *that is who I want to be*. We usually think of passion as an inner quality. But the more I visited hotbeds, the
more I saw it as something that came first from the outside
world. In the hotbeds the right butterfly wingflap was causing
talent hurricanes.

"I remember watching [Pak] on TV," said Christina Kim,
a South Korean–American golfer. "She wasn't blond or blue-
eyed, and we were of the same blood . . . You say to yourself,
'If she can do it, why can't I?'" Larisa Preobrazhenskaya, the
Spartak coach, remembers the moment when the spark
caught. "All the little girls started wearing their hair in pony-
tails and grunting when they hit," she said. "They were all little Annas."

Ignition is a strange concept because it burns just out of

our awareness, largely within our unconscious mind. But that doesn't mean it can't be captured, understood, and used to produce useful heat. In the next few chapters we'll see how our built-in ignition system works, and how tiny, seemingly insignificant cues can, over time, create gigantic differences in skill. We'll visit some places that have ignited, even though they might not know it, and we'll see how myelin is really made out of love. Let's begin by taking a closer look at the ignition process.

The Tiny, Powerful Idea

In 1997 Gary McPherson set out to investigate a mystery that has puzzled parents and music teachers since time immemorial: why certain children progress quickly at music lessons and others don't. He undertook a long-term study that sought to analyze the musical development of 157 randomly selected children. (This was the study that would generate the footage of Clarissa practicing the clarinet.) McPherson took a uniquely comprehensive approach, following the children from a few weeks before they picked out their instrument (at age seven or eight in most cases) through to high school graduation, tracking their progress through a detailed battery of interviews, biometric tests, and videotaped practice sessions.

After the first nine months of lessons the kids were a typical mixed bag: a few had zoomed off like rockets; a few had barely budged; most were somewhere in the middle. Skill was scattered along a bell curve of what we'd intuitively consider to be musical aptitude. The question was, what caused the curve? Was it inevitable, just a descriptive chart of what happens among any randomly chosen population who are striving to master a skill? Or was there some hidden X factor that explained and predicted each child's success and failure?

McPherson started analyzing his data to try to find the reason. Was the X factor IQ? Nope. Was it aural sensitivity? Nope. Was it math skills or sense of rhythm? Sensorimotor skills? Income level? Nope, nope, nope, nope.

Then McPherson tested a new factor: the children's answers to a simple question that he'd asked them *before* they had even started their first lesson. The question was, how long do you think you'll play your new instrument?

"They mostly say 'Uh, I dunno' at first ," McPherson said. "But then when you keep digging and ask them a few times, eventually they will give you a real solid answer. They have an idea, even then. They've picked up something in their environment that's made them say, yes, that's for me."

The children were asked to identify how long they planned to play (the options were: through this year, through primary school, through high school, all my life), and their answers were condensed into three categories:

Short-term commitment

Medium-term commitment

Long-term commitment

McPherson then measured how much each child practiced per week: low (20 minutes per week); medium (45 minutes per week); and high (90 minutes per week). He plotted the results against their performance on a skill test. The resulting graph looked like this:

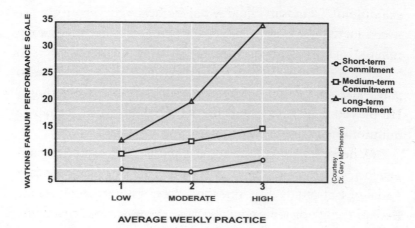

When McPherson saw the graph, he was stunned. "I couldn't believe my eyes," he said. Progress was determined not by any measurable aptitude or trait, but by a tiny, powerful idea the child had before even starting lessons. The differences were staggering. With the same amount of practice, the long-term-commitment group outperformed the short-term-commitment group by 400 percent. The long-term-commitment group, with a mere twenty minutes of weekly practice, progressed faster than the short-termers who practiced for an hour and a half. When long-term commitment combined with high levels of practice, skills skyrocketed.

"We instinctively think of each new student as a blank slate, but the ideas they bring to that first lesson are probably far more important than anything a teacher can do, or any amount of practice," McPherson said. "It's all about their perception of self. At some point very early on they had a crystallizing experience that brings the idea to the fore, that says, *I am a musician*. That idea is like a snowball rolling downhill."

To illustrate how this snowball works, McPherson used the

example of Clarissa. The day before her high-velocity practice, Clarissa's teacher had been trying to teach her a new song
called "La Cinquantaine." As usual with Clarissa, the lesson
had not gone well. Out of frustration, the teacher decided to
play a jazz version of "La Cinquantaine"—"Golden Wedding."
He played a few bars, and the whole thing took perhaps a
minute. But a minute was enough.

"When he played that, at that moment, something happened," McPherson said. "Clarissa was awestruck by the jazz
version. Entranced. She saw the teacher play it, and he must
have played with some style, because she got an image of herself as a performer. The teacher didn't realize it then, but
everything came together, and all of a sudden while hardly
knowing it, she's on fire, desperate to learn."

Note the process McPherson is describing here. The teacher's
playing caused Clarissa to experience an intense emotional response. That response—call it fascination, rapture, or love—
instantly connected Clarissa to a high-octane fuel tank of
motivation, which powered her deep practice. It's the same
thing that happened to the South Korean golfers and the
Russian tennis players. In their case, they used that fuel, over
a decade's time, to dominate two sports; in Clarissa's case, she
used that energy to accomplish a month's worth of practice in
six minutes.

McPherson's graph, like the table showing the rise of South
Korean golfers and Russian tennis players, is not a picture of
aptitude. It is a picture of ignition. What ignited the progress
wasn't any innate skill or gene. It was a small, ephemeral, yet
powerful idea: a vision of their ideal future selves, a vision that
oriented, energized, and accelerated progress, and that originated in the outside world. After all, these kids weren't born
wanting to be musicians. Their wanting, like Clarissa's, came

from a distinct signal, from something in their family, their homes, their teachers, the set of images and people they encountered in their short lives. That signal sparked an intense, nearly unconscious response that manifested itself as an idea: *I want to be like them*. It wasn't necessarily a logical idea for them to have. (Recall that it didn't correlate with any aural, rhythmic, or mathematic skills they possessed.) Perhaps the idea came about purely by accident. But accidents have consequences, and the consequence of this one was that they started out ignited, and that made all the difference.*

FLIPPING THE TRIGGER

Being highly motivated, when you think about it, is a slightly irrational state. One forgoes comfort now in order to work toward some bigger prospective benefit later on. It's not as simple as saying *I want X*. It's saying something far more complicated: *I want X later, so I better do Y like crazy right now.* We speak of motivation as if it's a rational assessment of cause and effect, but in fact it's closer to a bet, and a highly uncertain one at that. (What if the future benefits don't come?) This paradox is made plain in a scene in Mark Twain's *Tom Sawyer*.

Tom Sawyer is whitewashing a fence under strict orders

---

* At Meadowmount Music School I met a dozen kids who, when I asked them how they came to play, were vague, saying things like "I just always liked the violin/cello/piano." Then when I inquired what their parents did, it turned out that they played in symphony orchestras. In other words, these kids had spent hundreds of hours of their childhood watching the person they loved most in the world practice and perform classical music. In light of McPherson's study, this is ignition *in excelsis*. Speaking of parental cues, Meadowmount's roster included three Gabriels, named after the angel of music.

from his Aunt Polly. A neighborhood kid named Ben saunters past, teasingly informing Tom of his afternoon plans.

[Ben] "Say—I'm going in a-swimming, I am. Don't you wish you could? But of course you'd druther work—wouldn't you? Course you would!"

Tom contemplated the boy a bit, and said:

"What do you call work?"

"Why, ain't that work?"

Tom resumed his whitewashing, and answered carelessly:

"Well, maybe it is, and maybe it ain't. All I know is, it suits Tom Sawyer."

"Oh come, now, you don't mean to let on that you like it?"

The brush continued to move.

"Like it? Well, I don't see why I oughtn't to like it. Does a boy get a chance to whitewash a fence every day?"

That put the thing in a new light. Ben stopped nibbling his apple. Tom swept his brush daintily back and forth—stepped back to note the effect—added a touch here and there—criticized the effect again—Ben watching every move and getting more and more interested, more and more absorbed. Presently he said:

"Say, Tom, let me whitewash a little."

Tom considered, was about to consent; but he altered his mind:

"No—no—I reckon it wouldn't hardly do, Ben. You see, Aunt Polly's awful particular about this fence—right here on the street, you know—but if it was the back fence I wouldn't mind and she wouldn't. Yes, she's awful particular about this fence; it's got to be done very careful;

I reckon there ain't one boy in a thousand, maybe two
thousand, that can do it the way it's got to be done."

We all know what happens next: Ben is ignited, setting off
a contagion of motivation that ends with Tom happily observing as the neighborhood kids barter and beg for the
chance to whitewash the fence in his stead. Fiction though it
may be, the passage suggests the sorts of signals that work
best to ignite people.

The previous section contained three examples of ignition: South Korean/Russian athletes, mile runners, and beginner musicians. In each case, their ignition was reactive.
It may have *felt* like it originated within them, but in fact it
did not. In each case it was a response to a signal that arrived
in the form of an image: the victory of an older country-
woman, the barrier-smashing accomplishment of a fellow
runner, the unexpectedly captivating performance of a
teacher. The question is, what do these signals have in
common?

The answer is, each has to do with identity and groups, and
the links that form between them. Each signal is the motivational equivalent of a flashing red light: *those people over there*
are doing something terrifically worthwhile. Each signal, in
short, is about future belonging.

Future belonging is a primal cue: a simple, direct signal
that activates our built-in motivational triggers, funneling our
energy and attention toward a goal. The idea makes intuitive
sense—after all, we've all felt motivated by the desire to connect ourselves to high-achieving groups. What's interesting,
however, is just how powerful and unconscious those triggers
can be.

"We're the most social creatures on the planet," says Dr. Geoff Cohen of the University of Colorado. "Everything depends on collective effort and cooperation. When we get a cue that we ought to connect our identity with a group, it's like a hair trigger, like turning on a light switch. The ability to achieve is already there, but the energy put into that ability goes through the roof."

Cohen is one of a growing group of psychologists who specialize in uncovering the unconscious mechanisms that quietly govern our choices, motivations, and goals. Officially this area of study is called automaticity, but for our purposes Cohen and his colleagues are like the garage mechanics of ignition, tracing the invisible connections between our motivations and the environmental signals that quietly activate them. One of the rudimentary truths that the automaticity experts like to point out is that our motivational wiring isn't exactly new. In fact, most of the motivational circuits in our brains go back millions of years and are located in the area of the mind called the reptilian brain.

"Pursuing a goal, having motivation—all of that predates consciousness," said John Bargh, a psychologist at Yale University who pioneered automaticity studies in the mid-1980s. "Our brains are always looking for a cue as to where to spend energy now. Now? Now? We're swimming in an ocean of cues, constantly responding to them, but like fish in water, we just don't see it."

I asked Bargh about a curious pattern I'd observed at the talent hotbeds: they tended to be junky, unattractive places. If the training grounds of all the talent hotbeds I visited were magically assembled into a single facility—a mega-hotbed, as it were—that place would resemble a shantytown. Its buildings would be makeshift, corrugated-roofed affairs, its walls paint-bald, its fields weedy and uneven. So many hotbeds shared this disheveled ambience that I began to sense a link between the dented, beat-up state of the incubators and the sleek talent they produced. Which, in Bargh's opinion, was precisely the case, and for a reason he readily explained.

"If we're in a nice, easy, pleasant environment, we natu-rally shut off effort," Bargh said. "Why work? But if people get the signal that it's rough, they get motivated now. A nice, well-kept tennis academy gives them the luxury future right now—of course they'd be demotivated. They can't help it."

The research of Bargh and his colleagues adds up to a the-orem that might be dubbed the Scrooge Principle, which goes as follows: our unconscious mind is a stingy banker of energy reserves, keeping its wealth locked in a vault. Direct pleas to open the vault often don't work; Scrooge can't be fooled that easily. But when he's hit with the right combination of primal cues—when he's visited by a series of primal-cue ghosts, you might say—the tumblers click, the vault of energy flies open, and suddenly it's Christmas Day.

A few years ago Cohen and his colleague Gregory Walton tried to start their own motivation explosion. They took a group of Yale freshmen and gave them an innocuous mix of magazine articles to read. Included was a one-page first-person account of a student named Nathan Jackson. Jackson's story was brief: he had arrived at college not knowing what career to pursue, had developed a liking for math, and now had a happy career in a math department of a university. The story included a small biographical profile about Jackson: hometown, education, birth date. The article, like the others, was utterly forgettable—except for one microscopic detail: for half the students, Nathan Jackson's birth date was altered to exactly match the students' own. After they read the article, Cohen and Walton tested the students' attitudes toward math and measured their persistence; i.e., how long they were willing to work on an insoluble math problem.

When the results came in, Cohen and Walton found that the birthday-matched group had significantly more positive attitudes about math, and persisted a whopping 65 percent longer on the insoluble problem. What's more, those students did not feel any conscious change. The coincidence of the birthday, in Walton's phrase, "got underneath them."

"They were in a room by themselves taking the test. The door was shut; they were socially isolated; and yet [the birthday connection] had meaning for them," Walton said. "They weren't alone. The love and interest in math became part of them. They had no idea why. Suddenly it was *us* doing this, not just *me*.

"Our suspicion is that these events are powerful because they are small and indirect," Walton continued. "If we had told them this same information directly, if they had noticed it, it would have had less effect. It's not strategic; we don't think of it as being useful because we're not even thinking of it at all. It's automatic."

If the conceptual model for deep practice is a circuit being slowly wrapped with insulation, then the model for ignition is a hair trigger connected to a high-voltage power plant. Accordingly, ignition is determined by simple if/then propositions, with the *then* part always the same—*better get busy*. See someone you want to become? *Better get busy*. Want to catch up with a desirable group? *Better get busy*. Bargh and his colleagues have performed a number of similarly magical-seeming experiments, where they use tiny environmental cues (such as inspirational words hidden in a crossword puzzle) to manipulate motivation and effort among unknowing experimental subjects. They possess piles of supportive data to explain why this is so effective—for instance, the fact that the unconscious mind is able to process 11 million pieces of information per second, while the conscious mind can manage a mere 40. This disproportion points to the efficiency and necessity of relegating mental activities to the unconscious—and helps us to understand why appeals to the unconscious can be so effective.

One of the better demonstrations of the power of primal cues, however, came about by accident. In the 1970s, a clinical psychologist from Long Island named Martin Eisenstadt tracked the parental histories of every person who was eminent enough to have earned a half-page-long entry in the *Encyclopaedia Britannica*—a roster of 573 subjects, spanning Homer to John F. Kennedy, a rich mix of writers, scientists, political leaders, composers, soldiers, philosophers, and explorers. Eisenstadt wasn't interested in motivation per se; in fact, he was testing a theory he'd developed relating genius and psychosis to the loss of a parent or parents at an early age. But he wound up constructing an elegant demonstration of the relationship between motivation and primal cues.

Within this accomplished group the parental-loss club turned out to be standing room only. Political leaders who lost a parent at an early age include Julius Caesar (father, 15), Napoleon (father, 15), fifteen British prime ministers, Washington (father, 11), Jefferson (father, 14), Lincoln (mother, 9), Lenin (father, 15), Hitler (father, 13), Gandhi (father, 15),

Stalin (father, 11), and (we reflexively paste in) Bill Clinton (father, infant). Scientists and artists on the list include Copernicus (father, 10), Newton (father, before birth), Darwin (mother, 8), Dante (mother, 6), Michelangelo (mother, 6), Bach (mother and father, 9), Handel (father, 11), Dostoyevsky (mother, 15), Keats (father, 8; mother, 14), Byron (father, 3), Emerson (father, 8), Melville (father, 12), Wordsworth (mother, 7; father, 13), Nietzsche (father, 4), Charlotte, Emily, and Anne Brontë (mother at 5, 3, and 1, respectively), Woolf (mother, 13), and Twain (father, 11). On average, the eminent group lost their first parent at an average age of 13.9, compared with 19.6 for a control group. All in all, it's a list deep and broad enough to justify the question posed by a 1978 French study: *do orphans rule the world?**

The genetic explanation for world-class achievement is useless in this case, because the people on this list are linked by

---

* For the sake of updating Eisenstadt, here's a partial list of show business stars who lost a parent before the age of eighteen: **Comedy:** Steve Allen (1, father), Tim Allen (11, father), Lucille Ball (3, father), Mel Brooks (2, father), Drew Carey (8, father), Charlie Chaplin (12, father), Stephen Colbert (10, father), Billy Crystal (15, father), Eric Idle (6, father), Eddie Izzard (6, father), Bernie Mac (16, mother), Eddie Murphy (8, father), Rosie O'Donnell (11, mother), Molly Shannon (4, mother), Martin Short (17, mother), Red Skelton (infant, father), Tom and Dick Smothers (7 and 8, father), Tracey Ullman (6, father), Fred Willard (11, father). **Music:** Louis Armstrong, Tony Bennett, 50 Cent, Aretha Franklin, Bob Geldof, Robert Goulet, Isaac Hayes, Jimi Hendrix, Madonna, Charlie Parker. The ignition effect seems to be present in the Beatles (Paul McCartney, 14, mother, and John Lennon, 17, mother) and U2 (Bono, 14, mother, and Larry Mullen, 15, mother). **Movies:** Cate Blanchett, Orlando Bloom, Mia Farrow, Jane Fonda, Daniel Day-Lewis, Sir Ian McKellen, Robert Redford, Julia Roberts, Martin Sheen, Barbra Streisand, Charlize Theron, Billy Bob Thornton, Benicio del Toro, James Woods. This list doesn't, of course, include those who lost contact with a parent as the result of divorce, illness, or some other factor, a list that would fill a book in itself. One of the clearest expressions of the way loss causes ignition comes from composer-producer Quincy Jones, whose mother suffered from schizophrenia. "I never felt like I had a mother," he said. "I used to sit in the closet and say, 'If I don't have a mother, I don't need one. I'm going to make music and creativity my mother.' It never let me down. Never."

shared life events that have nothing to do with chromosomes. But when we look at parental loss as a signal hitting a motivational trigger, the connection becomes clearer. Losing a parent is a primal cue: *you are not safe*. You don't have to be a psychologist to appreciate the massive outpouring of energy that can be created by a lack of safety; nor do you have to be a Darwinian theorist to appreciate how such a response might have evolved. This signal can alter the child's relationship to the world, redefine his identity, and energize and orient his mind to address the dangers and possibilities of life—a response Eisenstadt summed up as "a springboard of immense compensatory energy." Or as Dean Keith Simonton wrote of parental loss in *Origins of Genius*, "[S]uch adverse events nurture the development of a personality robust enough to overcome the many obstacles and frustrations standing in the path of achievement."

If we take it one step further and presume that many of the world-class scientists, artists, and writers on Eisenstadt's list accomplished the requisite ten thousand hours of deep practice, the mechanism of their ignition becomes more apparent. Losing a parent at a young age was not what gave them talent; rather, it was the primal cue—*you are not safe*—that, by tripping the ancient self-preserving evolutionary switch, provided energy for their efforts, so that they built their various talents over the course of years, step by step, wrap by wrap. Seen this way, the superstars on Eisenstadt's list are not uniquely gifted exceptions, but rather the logical extensions of the same universal principles that govern all of us: (1) talent requires deep practice; (2) deep practice requires vast amounts of energy; (3) primal cues trigger huge outpourings of energy. And as George Bartzokis might point out, the eminent people, on average, received this signal as young teens, during the brain's key development period, in which information-processing pathways are particularly receptive to myelin.*

   The second example of ignition originates a little closer to home. In our family of six, our daughter Zoe is the youngest and, for her age (seven), the speediest. Her foot speed seems perfectly natural, and yet since I started learning about myelin, I began to wonder how much of Zoe's foot speed is innate, and how much of it stems from the combination of practice and motivation she gets from being the youngest?
   I undertook a highly unscientific survey of my friends' children. The pattern seemed to hold: the youngest kids were frequently the fastest runners. It became more interesting when I broadened the sample group slightly. Here are the birth-order ranks of the world-record progression in the 100-meter dash, with the most recently set world record first, the previous world record second, and so on.

   1. Usain Bolt (second of three children)
   2. Asafa Powell (sixth of six)
   3. Justin Gatlin (fourth of four)
   4. Maurice Greene (fourth of four)
   5. Donovan Bailey (third of three)
   6. Leroy Burrell (fourth of five)
   7. Carl Lewis (third of four)

---

* Of course, a parent's death or absence doesn't always lead to talent or achievement. The same event can be debilitating—hence Eisenstadt's link to psychosis—or, in cases where the deceased parent was abusive, an improvement in the child's life. The point of Eisenstadt's list is proportion: that people who lose a parent at a young age, on the whole, have more opportunity, means, and motive to use that immense compensatory energy to grow myelin and skill. Whether they use it to become John Lennon or John Wilkes Booth is a matter of fate and circumstance.

8. Burrell (fourth of five)
9. Lewis (third of four)
10. Calvin Smith (sixth of eight)

While the sample size is small, the pattern is clear. Of the eight men on the list (Burrell and Lewis appear twice), none of them were firstborn, and only one was born in the first half of his family's birth order. In all, history's fastest runners were born, on average, fourth in families of 4.6 children. We find a similar result with the top-ten all-time NFL running backs in rushing yardage, who score an average birth rank of 3.2 out of families of 4.4 kids.

This pattern strikes us as surprising, because speed looks like a gift. It feels like a gift. And yet this pattern suggests that speed is not purely a gift but a skill that grows through deep practice, and that is ignited by primal cues. In this case the cue is: *you're behind—keep up!* We can safely imagine that in most families this signal is sent and received hundreds if not thousands of times over the childhood years, sent by older, bigger kids to smaller, younger ones, who respond with levels of effort and intensity that those older children (who share the same genetic inheritance) never had the opportunity to experience. (And recall that myelin is all about impulse speed: the more you have, the faster your muscles can fire—a particularly handy feature for sprinters.)

This is not to say that being born late into a big family automatically makes someone fast, any more than having a parent die early in life automatically makes one prime minister of England. But it does say that being fast, like any talent, involves a confluence of factors that go beyond genes and that are directly related to the intense, subconscious reaction to motivational signals that provide the energy to practice deeply and thus grow myelin. As with McPherson's musicians, the South Korean golfers, and the Russian tennis players, Zoe and the rest of the people on this list are talented not only because they were born that way but also because at some mysterious point they caught on to a powerful idea, an idea that originated in the flow of images and signals around them, those tiny sparks that set them alight. *Skill is insulation that wraps neural circuits and grows according to certain signals.*

O LUCKY ME!

Safety and future belonging are two powerful primal cues. But they are not the only ones useful for igniting talent.

In the early 1980s a young violin teacher named Roberta Tzavaras decided to bring classical music to three Harlem public elementary schools. The problem was, there were far more students than violins. To solve this problem, as well as to underscore her belief that every child is capable of learning to play the violin, Tzavaras decided to hold a lottery. The first class, made up of the lottery winners, made surprisingly fast progress. So did the second, and the third. The program thrived and came to be called the Opus 118 Harlem Center for Strings. Tzavaras and her students have performed at Carnegie Hall, at Lincoln Center, and on *The Oprah Winfrey Show*. Their success inspired a documentary film, *Small Wonders,* and a 1999 Hollywood movie called *Music of the Heart*.

Naturally, other public schools attempted to develop their own versions of Opus 118, among them two public schools: Wadleigh Secondary School of the Performing and Visual Arts in Harlem, and PS 233 in Flatbush, Brooklyn. The two violin programs make a useful comparison because they started at about the same time and happened to be taught by the same instructor, David Burnett of the Harlem School for the Arts. They also make a useful comparison because one of the programs succeeded and the other did not.

To predict beforehand which program would succeed might seem easy. Wadleigh enjoyed numerous advantages over PS 233, including an arts-focused curriculum, parents who had, by enrolling their child, expressed a belief in the value of art education, students who presumably had a real interest in music, a brand-new auditorium, and a budget that permitted the school to purchase violins for every student who wanted to play. PS 233, on the other hand, was an archetypal urban public school. The students had no apparent inclination toward violins or arts in general. What's more, the foundation that funded the program could afford only fifty violins, most of which were too small, forcing Burnett to hold an Opus 118–style lottery to determine who got in. As the programs got under way, the result seemed preordained: Wadleigh would succeed, and PS 233 would fail.

And yet, a year later, it was the Wadleigh program that was sputtering and the PS 233 program that was going strong. The Wadleigh program was beset with discipline problems, and the PS 233 group was well behaved. The Wadleigh students teased the good players and discouraged them from continuing, and the PS 233 students did their practice and got steadily better. When asked to explain, Burnett can only say that the Wadleigh program "just failed to take off."

Why? I believe part of the answer can be found in *Small Wonders*, the documentary film on Opus 118. Early in the film, its makers capture the scene of Tzavaras visiting a first-grade class to perform music and tell them about a group to which they might someday belong—if they are fortunate. As she explains how the lottery works, the kids bounce up and down nervously; they clamor for applications to take home to their parents. A week or two goes by; a sense of anticipation builds. Tzavaras returns to the classroom carrying a stack of winning applications. Then, to rapt silence, she proceeds to announce the winners' names. On hearing their names, the kids react as if they'd just received an electric shock. They dance. They scream. They flail their arms in joy. They race home to tell their parents the thrilling news: they won! They don't know the A string from the A train, but it doesn't matter in the least. Like the long-term commitment group in Gary McPherson's study, they are ignited, and it makes all the difference.

If talent is a gift sprinkled randomly through the world's children, we would naturally expect Wadleigh's program to be the one to succeed. But if talent is a process that can be ignited by primal cues, then the reason for PS 233's success is clear. The genetic potential in both schools was the same; the teaching was the same; the difference was, the students at Wadleigh received the motivational equivalent of a gentle nudge, while the PS 233 students were ignited by primal cues of scarcity and belonging. In each case the kids reacted the same way any of us would.

Let's return to the question that started the previous section. Why was Tom Sawyer able to persuade Ben to help him whitewash the fence? The answer is that Tom flung primal cues at Ben with the speed and accuracy of a circus knife-thrower. In the space of a few sentences, he managed to hit bull's-eyes of exclusivity ("All I know is, it suits Tom Sawyer . . . I reckon there ain't one boy in a thousand . . .") and scarcity ("Does a boy get a chance to whitewash a fence every day? . . . Aunt Polly's awful particular about this fence"). His gestures and body language echoed the same messages: he "contemplated the boy a bit," and "stepped back to note the effect—added a touch here and there—criticized the effect again," as though engaged in a work of the greatest importance. If Tom had only sent one or two of these signals, or if they'd been spaced over the course of a leisurely hour, his cues would have had no effect; Ben's trigger would have remained untouched. But the rich combination of cues, peppering Ben's ignition switch one after another, succeeded in cracking open his vault of motivational energy.

We usually regard this passage as an example of a sophisticated con job: clever Tom Sawyer hoodwinking gullible yokels into doing unsavory work. Primal-cue psychology allows us to see it in a slightly different way. Tom's signals worked not because Ben was some thoughtless dupe. (Indeed, a thoughtless dupe would have shrugged and trudged on to the swimming hole.) Tom's signals worked because Ben, as Twain wrote, was "watching every move" and was "absorbed." Ben's was the response of an attentive kid who saw in Tom Sawyer's work something attractive and who was ignited—not unlike the response of attentive kids in South Korea or Russia, or of Zoe watching her siblings run ahead of her. Ignition doesn't follow normal rules because it's not designed to follow rules. It's designed only to work, to give us energy for whatever tasks we choose—or, as we'll see next, for whatever tasks fate chooses for us.

Chapter 6

The Curaçao Experiment

The whole island jumped.
—Lucio Anthonia, Curaçao Little League parent

THE EARTHQUAKE

Every August at the Little League World Series in Williamsport, Pennsylvania, a team of eleven- and twelve-year-old boys from Curaçao stages a vivid reenactment of David versus Goliath. Actually, it's more like David versus fifteen Goliaths. In a sixteen-team tournament frequently dominated by hulking, flame-throwing man-boys, this wiry, undersize team of nobodies from a tiny, remote Caribbean island somehow keeps succeeding.* In a worldwide competition where qualifying two consecutive years is considered a remarkable achievement, the Curaçao boys have made it to the semifinals six times in the last eight years, winning the title in

* In 2007 the average player from the American Midwest team stood five feet seven and weighed 136 pounds. Curaçao's average player was five feet one inches tall and weighed 106 pounds.

2004 and finishing second in 2005. As ESPN announcers have christened it, Curaçao is the Little Island That Could.

Curaçao's accomplishments are even more impressive for the fact that compared with the teams they beat, they have precious few facilities. (There are only two Little League–regulation fields on the entire island, and one batting cage constructed of tattered fishnet.) What's more, the Curaçao baseball season lasts but five months; practices are held three times a week, and games are on weekends, a schedule that contrasts markedly with the year-round approach of other places like Venezuela. When I saw them in Williamsport at the 2007 series, the younger members of the Curaçao team were bemused by the spectacle of the Japanese team doing drills before breakfast. ("Why do they do *that*?" one player asked me, mystified.)

The most compelling element of this underdog story, however, is that Curaçao's success can be traced to a single moment of ignition—actually two moments, lasting approximately three seconds each. They both happened at Yankee Stadium on October 20, 1996, in the opening game of the World Series between the Atlanta Braves and the New York Yankees. Like many moments of ignition, this one fascinates because it hangs so heavily on chance, literally on the postage-stamp-size area of contact created when a round bat meets a round ball. One-eighth of an inch either way, and, if history is any guide, the Curaçao phenomenon would not have happened.

The situation at Yankee Stadium seemed unpromising: no score, top of the second inning, Braves runner on first base. An unknown nineteen-year-old Curaçaoan rookie named Andruw Jones stood at the plate waggling his bat, a Mona Lisa smile creasing his chubby face. Jones had started his season at the single-A level of the minor leagues; he'd been promoted to the majors only two months earlier. The Yankee ace, Andy Pettitte, stared him down with the somber expression of a bullfighter. Pettitte was only a few years older but in this image the narrative was clear: canny veteran versus naïve rookie.

Pettitte worked the count full, then unleashed his best pitch: a nasty slider. The intention was to induce the rookie to do what most rookies do in that situation: get fooled, reach for the pitch, and ground it into a double play. But Jones was not most rookies. Jones recognized the spin on the slider and slammed the pitch ten rows into the left-field seats. Fifty-six thousand Yankee fans went quiet as Jones, his smile broadening, sped around the bases.

It was an extraordinary feat, one that couldn't possibly be outdone. But then it was. The very next inning Jones walked up to the plate and, on another full-count pitch, smashed an even more towering drive into the left-field seats. The television announcers gasped and stammered as if solving a difficult mathematical equation: World Series plus Yankee Stadium plus unknown teenager equals *two* consecutive home runs? A nuclear burst of media attention followed, hailing Jones's natural-born talent, comparing him to Clemente, Mantle, and da Vinci, marveling at the unearthly God-given quickness of his wrists. (In fact, that quickness was no gift from above. Jones had been swinging a bat since the age of two, coached by his father, Henry. When he was older, Andruw swung a sledgehammer three times a week, rolling his wrists in a circle to build hand speed and strength. As Jones later put it, "[My dad] taught me baseball stuff: to work my ass off.") The Hall of Fame in Cooperstown requested Jones's bat. Agence France-Presse called it the "greatest debut in World Series history." Like a shock wave, Jones's historic feat flashed on screens around the world.

But all that was nothing compared to the blast that rocked Jones's hometown of Willemstad. Curaçao's Little League founder, Frank Curiel, remembers the sound he heard when Jones hit the home runs. "It was very, very loud. Firecrackers, yelling, everyone shouting, everyone waking up." A few weeks later at Little League sign-ups the first aftershock showed up in the form of four hundred new kids. Their motivation was perhaps all the stronger since they knew that Jones hadn't even been one of the best players on the island. As a fifteen-year-old he had switched from third base to outfield so he could get more playing time. (After all, if *he* could do it...)*

Even with this extraordinary infusion of enthusiastic recruits, Curaçao's talent bloom took time to develop, just as it did for Russia's tennis players and South Korea's golfers—after all, myelin doesn't grow overnight. Not until 2001, five years after Jones's home runs, did a team of Curaçao Little Leaguers arrive at Howard J. Lamade Stadium in Williamsport to compete in the Little League World Series (LLWS). Tournament officials considered it a fluke appearance. After all, Curaçao had qualified for the LLWS only once before, back in 1980, and as LLWS press officer Christopher Downs put it, "[Curaçao] had always been pretty miserable." But the

---

* Interestingly, the same pattern occurred among mile runners in their reaction to the success of Roger Bannister, who wasn't considered among the world's talents when he broke the four-minute mark. Similarly, Anna Kournikova had been routinely defeated by many of her tennis teammates. The peers' reaction in both cases was to be incredulous and highly motivated at once: *Them?*

Curaçao team, half of which had originally signed up after Jones's homers, surprised observers by reaching the international final. Though they lost 2–1 to the eventual champions from Tokyo, they had succeeded at establishing the giant-slayer plotline that they've faithfully followed ever since.

As is true of any talent hotbed, Curaçao's success wasn't caused solely by the primal signals that created ignition. The matrix of other causes includes disciplined culture, top-notch coaching, supportive parents, national pride, the love of the game, and of course, a wealth of deep practice. (From what I saw, Jones's style of training is the rule, not the exception.)

Curaçao is interesting for another reason: a few dozen miles west lies the island of Aruba. Aruba is like Curaçao in almost every measurable way. They have the same population, the same language, the same Dutch-influenced culture, and the same love of baseball; even their flags are nearly carbon copies. Aruba fields quality Little League teams that, until recently, competed well against Curaçao's. To top it off, Aruba had even produced a major-league player who was, for a moment in 1996, regarded as a better prospect than Andruw Jones. That star's name was Sidney Ponson, and his early success with the Baltimore Orioles, like that of Jones with the Braves, had fueled Aruban Little League with a fresh spark of excitement and participation. The two islands were twins, right down to the motivational spark, and yet Curaçao ignited while Aruba did not. Why?

Part of the answer is that Curaçao, like other talent hotbeds, has found a way to do a very important and tricky thing: to keep the motivational fire lit. It's one thing to persuade Scrooge to crack open his vault; it's another to persuade him to splurge on Christmas geese day after day, year after year. Curaçao forms, quite by accident, a natural case study on the science and practice of sustained ignition.

THE SISTINE CHAPEL EFFECT

Ignition, in Curaçao or anywhere, doesn't come with guarantees. For every breakthrough performance that ignites a talent bloom, there are dozens of breakthroughs that peter out. Germany's Boris Becker won Wimbledon at seventeen but inspired no Teutonic wave of players. Miguel Cervantes dazzled the Shakespearean era with *Don Quixote* but had little apparent effect in his native Spain. The painter Edvard Munch (*The Scream*) remains the sole member of that oxymoronic group, Norwegian expressionists. These cases, and others like them, lead us to an interesting question: why do breakthrough performances sometimes ignite talent blooms, and sometimes not?

The answer is that talent hotbeds possess more than a single primal cue. They contain complex collections of signals— people, images, and ideas—that keep ignition going for the weeks, months, and years that skill-growing requires. Talent hotbeds are to primal cues what Las Vegas is to neon signs, flashing with the kind of signals that keep motivation burning.

Consider the sights that a young Michelangelo would have encountered in a single afternoon in Florence. In a half-hour's stroll he could have visited the workshops of a dozen great artists. These were not quiet studios: to the contrary, they were beehives overseen by a master and a hustling team of journeymen and apprentices, competing for commissions, filling orders, making plans, testing new techniques. He could have encountered Donatello's Saint Mark statue, Ghiberti's

Gates of Paradise, the works of painters from his boss Ghirlandaio through Masaccio, Giotto, and Cimabue—the greatest hits of architecture, painting, and sculpture. All of them were concentrated within a few blocks; all of them were simply part of the landscape of everyday life; and all flashed signals that added up to one energizing message: *better get busy*.

Or consider the scene at the Mermaid Tavern in London during Shakespeare's day. There, across the river from the Globe Theatre, the major writers of the day—Marlowe, Jonson, Donne, Raleigh—gathered to talk shop and match wits. Or consider the Academy and Lyceum of Athens, where Plato, Aristotle, and the rest taught, argued, and learned. Or consider the thronging environs of São Paolo, where, walking around one afternoon, I attempted to keep track of the number of signals about soccer I spotted: a TV highlight, a billboard, an overheard conversation, four futsal pickup games, five kids juggling balls down the street. I lost track somewhere after fifty.

Frank Curiel Field in Willemstad, Curaçao, doesn't look much like ancient Greece. It has dented aluminum bleachers, a snack shack behind home plate, and on the day I've come to watch practice, a sprinkling of parents sipping Cokes and shooting the breeze. The teams are warming up for a game, playing catch, kidding around. It looks like a slightly more decrepit version of every small-town baseball field you've ever seen. But that's only camouflage. In fact, when I examine it more closely, I see that it's cluttered with primal cues.

The first cue stands six feet tall, wears an immaculate floral shirt, and carries a small red cup filled with Dewar's and Red Bull. This is Frank Curiel himself, the sixty-eight-year-old league founder, groundskeeper, scheduler, seller of the

Cokes, controller of the lights, keeper of the trophies, and benign ruler of this tiny kingdom. He is a tropical Don Corleone, a resemblance underlined by his hoarse whisper of a voice. Curiel shows me around his field, outlining his story as we walk: how he brought Little League to the island forty-five years ago, how he saw the great Clemente play in Puerto Rico, how he decided to start a league, how he went to Springfield College in Massachusetts to learn physical education, how he got a job with Curaçao's sports and recreation agency, how he would drive around Willemstad's neighborhoods to recruit kids to play.

"They played," he says. "Then their kids played, and now *their* kids play. I see them all."

In describing devoted organizers like Curiel, it's customary to state that they "live at the field." With Curiel, this is no figure of speech. His home is a ten-by-twelve-foot tin-roofed shack that sits atop steel pilings just behind home plate; a swatch of chain-link fence prevents foul balls from flying into his soup. The room is a riotous flood of trophies, plaques, equipment, and photos, which threaten to overrun the bed and the television that are among Curiel's few concessions to domesticity. Curiel is always around, watching, raking the field, running the lights, keeping the kids in line. Below, on a porch that serves as a Wall of Fame, Curiel has posted more photos of the greatest moments in the island's base-ball history. Some nights Curiel sets up the television on the porch so the kids can gather and watch big-league games or, as happens often, a scratchy videotape of Andruw Jones's homers.

With a princely gaze, Curiel surveys his domain. "To play ball, you need three things," he pronounces, touching his body as if doing the sign of the cross. "Heart. Mind. Balls. If you have two, you can play, but you will never be great. To be great, all three."

We walk around the field. Near third base Curiel stops to correct a small boy fielding a grounder. He speaks in a burst of Papiamento, the native language, which sounds like a reggae record played backward at high speed. Curiel is telling the boy to move in front of the ball. "Like this," he demonstrates, setting down his Dewar's, scooping an imaginary ball, and firing it to an invisible base. "Like this! Yes!" The boy watches, nods, and does it.

Behind the backstop, seated at a cement table, are two men talking into small headsets. They are preparing the weekly radio broadcast of the game on Curaçao radio, via a homemade setup. Next to them stands a man in a red baseball cap. His name is Fermin Coronel, and he's a scout for the St. Louis Cardinals, one of several big-league scouts who live on the island. Around them sit the parents, whose casual demeanor belies their detailed knowledge of tactics and history. "Watch this boy, he has a good change-up," a fifty-something mother warns me. Another man tells me of his eleven-year-old son's private workouts, which include jogging three times a week and using dumbbells to build core strength. "It's the same workout Jurrjens used," the father says, referring to Jair Jurrjens, a highly regarded second-year pitcher with the Atlanta Braves whose father, by the way, is standing just over there, by the backstop.

Then there are the kids. At the top of this loose hierarchy are the older teens who play junior-league ball and help coach. Many of them have been to Williamsport and still wear their battered LLWS caps as badges of honor. Then come waves of increasingly younger kids, the ones for whom the LLWS is a fresh memory, the ones who return telling stories of jet flights and plasma televisions, of getting to meet major-league stars and seeing themselves on ESPN. Then come the ones who are trying to make the all-star team this year (they're the most serious of all), and finally the loose packs of four- and five-year-olds who tumble in and out of the proceedings like so many kittens, watchful and quick.

Frank Curiel Field is not so much a field as a window through which these kids can see the ascending realms of heaven stacked above them in neat levels, as in a medieval painting. First comes making the league all-star team (being one of *those* guys). Then comes Williamsport in all its celebrity glory (being one of *those* guys). Then just above that is getting signed by a scout, playing in the major leagues (being one of *those* guys). For the kids at Frank Curiel Field, these are not gauzy dreams or glossy posters; they are tangible steps on a primal ladder of selection,* distinct possibilities reflected in the crackle of the radio, the clutter of the trophies, the chrome glint off the major-league scout's sunglasses. (See that house down the street, the one with the nice SUV in the driveway? That's Andruw Jones's mom's house!) To be a six-year-old at this field is, motivationally speaking, sort of like standing in the Sistine Chapel. The proof of paradise is right here: all you have to do is open your eyes.

Late one evening in Curaçao I was driving around Wil-

---

* The most vivid example of the power of selection I came across was from 1987 at Spartak Tennis Club. The coach, Rauza Islanova, started her class with twenty-five seven-year-olds. Every second week or so she would reduce it by one. Of the seven who made the final selection, three became world-top-ten players (Elena Dementieva, Anastasia Myskina, and Marat Safin). "Not bad for one class," Dementieva said.

lemstad with Philbert Llewellyn. Like most of the adults around Curaçao Little League, Llewellyn had several jobs: coach, color announcer on the radio broadcast, and lieutenant in the police department. Around eight P.M. Llewellyn's cell phone rang, and I assumed it was police business. In fact, it was two of his ballplayers, who desperately needed him to settle an important bet about an obscure baseball rule. Llewellyn rendered his decision (no, the batter does not get credit for a sacrifice if the runner on second tags and goes to third), hung up, and smiled apologetically. "That happens a lot," he said.

I have coached Little League baseball off and on for more than a decade now, and I've received calls from players wanting to know about schedules, uniform numbers, and pizza parties, not to mention the occasional player who has a crush on my wife and wonders if maybe he can talk to her. But I've yet to get a phone call from two players arguing over the finer points of the sacrifice-fly rule.

"They are thinking about baseball," Llewellyn said with a policeman's knowing shrug. "All the time, it's going around and around inside their heads."

Let's return to the question with which we began: Why did Curaçao succeed in starting a hotbed while Aruba failed? Why, given the equality of gene pool, culture, and inspirational spark, didn't Aruba ignite? Beyond the factors already noted, we should also consider the fate of their respective igniters. Sidney Ponson, the Aruban pitcher who was such a marvelous prospect, turned out to have a drinking problem. He became overweight, bounced around to several teams, and on Christmas Day 2004 was arrested for assault and ordered to take part in twenty-seven hours of anger-management classes. Andruw Jones, on the other hand, became a five-time all-star and ten-time Gold Glove centerfielder. The larger reason, however, is that Curaçao possessed a set of tools to keep the ignition of Jones's success lit. Curaçao grew talent because the message of Jones's success was translated and amplified into a reliable combination of primal cues. Frank Curiel Field, after all, only looks like a beat-up baseball diamond. It is in fact a million-watt antenna steadily transmitting a powerful stream of signals and images that add up to a thrilling whisper: *Hey, that could be you.*

THE LANGUAGE OF IGNITION

Thus far we've learned a few things about the nature of our ignition switch. First, it's either on or off. Second, it can be triggered by certain signals, or primal cues. Now we'll look more deeply into how it can be triggered by the signals we use most: words.

As experts in motivational psychology go, Skip Engblom does not fit the usual mold. He is a big, shambling libertarian skate-shop owner from Santa Monica, California. Engblom, you might recall, helped found the Z-Boys skateboarding team. The mumbly, mercurial genius-stoner quintessence of his personality was captured by Heath Ledger in *Lords of Dogtown*, the feature film about the Z-Boys. The years have left Engblom largely unchanged, except for two things. First, his once-shaggy locks have been replaced by a gleaming Buddha dome. Second, he's gained new insights into his role in the Z-Boys' evolution from their random beginnings to their storied triumph at the 1975 Del Mar skateboard contest, insights that resonate best if he explains them himself. Here's the setup to his story: it's the early 1970s, and a handful of sketchy-looking kids start hanging around Engblom's surf shop after school.

"I saw them, but I didn't say anything at first. First, I wanted to make sure they weren't shoplifting or something, but when I saw they were being cool, I let them be. Everybody else would have kicked them out. But they were okay. I grew up without a dad, and I knew their deal; they kind of reminded me of me, you know what I mean?" In Engblomese, this last phrase comes out *unowaime?* "So we started spending time. It wasn't much, we went to the beach, surfed, I fed them. I saw they were really good surfers, some of these guys, so we entered this contest.

"So this one Saturday the contest comes along and there's this guy who was supposed to be The Guy, *unowaime?* He's some bigshot ringer dude who's going to turn pro or something. So I'm like the coach, right, and so I decide to put our smallest surfer, this little kid named Jay Adams, up against this pro guy in the first heat. Jay was thirteen. I knew Jay could do it, but Jay didn't know he could, he had no idea. So we're standing there getting ready for the contest, and people are gathered around, and they're freaking out that Jay and this guy are going to surf against each other. They're saying '*Whoa*, no way.' So that's when I go up to this bigshot pro guy, right where Jay can hear me, I tell the guy, 'Don't worry, bud. You don't stand a chance.'

"And Jay goes out and *slaughters* the guy. Jay beats the guy who was supposed to be The Guy. That's when everything changed. The kids saw that and went, *whoa*. We started getting good at that moment, they felt it. They took that to the waves and to the street when we started that up. And Jay was the one who had the idea, you know? The one who said we should start a skateboard team.

"When it came to skateboards, we got all systematic about it, practiced a couple hours a day, four days a week. There's no instant gratification, man. Everything boils back down to training; doing it over and over. So I never said much. I would just be mellow and say 'good job, dude' or 'nice shred,' and sometimes something to up the ante, toss in a little carrot, you know, like 'I heard so-and-so did that trick last week.' And then they'd all be trying like crazy to do that one, *unowaime?* Because they wanted to be part of the equation.

"When they showed up at that contest in Del Mar, everybody made it seem like it was some big surprise. But [the Z-Boys] knew exactly what was going to happen. They knew because they knew exactly how good they were, because they were trained up, because they *knew*. Not because I told them they could. But I helped them get there, definitely."

Engblom pauses, thinks deeply, and issues his wisdom.

"Here's the deal. You've got to give kids credit at a younger age for feeling stuff more acutely. When you say something to a kid, you've got to know what you're saying to them. The stuff you say to a kid starting out—you got to be supercareful, *unowaime?* What skill-building really is, is confidence-building. First they got to earn it, then they got it. And once it gets lit, it stays lit pretty good."

On one level Engblom didn't do all that much. His communications with the team consisted of a few mumbled phrases. Some of them set up a highly specific challenge at key moments ("Don't worry, bro, you don't have a chance"; "I heard so-and-so did that trick last week"). Others encouraged their efforts ("good job, dude"; "nice shred"). And yet without Engblom—without his verbal signals and his guidance—

the Z-Boys might never have happened, much less succeeded. It's as if those few offhand phrases, small as they were, somehow helped ignite them to new levels of motivation and effort.

And according to theories developed by Dr. Carol Dweck, Engblom's verbal cues, however minimal, are just the kind to send the right signal. Dweck is a social psychologist at Stanford who has spent the past thirty years studying motivation. She's carved an impressively varied path across the field, starting with animal motivation and shifting to more complex creatures, chiefly elementary and high school students. Some of her most eye-opening research involves the relationship between motivation and language. "Left to our own devices, we go along in a pretty stable mindset," she said. "But when we get a clear cue, a message that sends a spark, then *boing*, we respond."

The *boing* phenomenon can be seen most vividly in a series of experiments Dweck did with four hundred New York fifth graders. The study was a scientific version of the fable "The Princess and the Pea." Its goal was to see how much a tiny signal—a single sentence of praise—can affect performance and effort, and what kind of signal is most effective.

First, Dweck gave every child a test that consisted of fairly easy puzzles. Afterward the researcher informed all the children of their scores, adding a single six-word sentence of praise. Half of the kids were praised for their intelligence ("You must be smart at this"), and half were praised for their effort ("You must have worked really hard").

The kids were tested a second time, but this time they were offered a choice between a harder test and an easier test. Ninety percent of the kids who'd been praised for their effort chose the harder test. A majority of the kids who'd been praised for their intelligence, on the other hand, chose the easy test. Why? "When we praise children for their intelligence," Dweck wrote, "we tell them that's the name of the game: look smart, don't risk making mistakes."

The third level of tests was uniformly harder; none of the kids did well. However, the two groups of kids—the praised-for-effort group and the praised-for-intelligence group—responded very differently to the situation. "[The effort group] dug in and grew very involved with the test, trying solutions, testing strategies," Dweck said. "They later said they liked it. But the group praised for its intelligence hated the harder test. They took it as proof they weren't smart."

The experiment then came full circle, returning to a test of the same difficulty as the initial test. The praised-for-effort group improved their initial score by 30 percent, while the praised-for-intelligence group's score declined by 20 percent. All because of six short words. Dweck was so surprised at the result that she reran the study five times. Each time the result was the same.

"We are exquisitely attuned to messages telling us what is valued," Dweck said. "I think we go around all the time looking, looking, trying to understand, 'Who am I in this setting? Who am I in this framework?' So that when a clear message comes, it can send a spark."

True to the findings of Dweck's study, each of the hotbeds I visited used language that affirmed the value of effort and slow progress rather than innate talent or intelligence. At Spartak, for instance, they did not "play" tennis—they preferred the verb borot'sya—"fight" or "struggle." South Korean golfers are exhorted to yun sup'he, which translates (to Nike's possible delight) as "just do it." In Curaçao the nine-to ten-year olds play in the Liga Vraminga, the Little Ant League; the watchword is *progresa*, "baby steps." In Brazilian soccer the age levels are the Bottle (five- and six-year olds), Diapers (seven and eight), and Pacifier (nine and ten). The under-twenty national team is called the Aspirantes, the Hopeful Ones. ("The English call their youth team the Reserves!" Emilio Miranda told me, chortling. "What are they reserved for?") At all the places I visited, praise was not constant but was given only when it was earned—a finding that dovetails with the research of Dweck, who notes that motivation does not increase with increased levels of praise but often dips. "Remember, our study showed the effect that just six words can have," Dweck said. "It's all about clarity."

When we use the term *motivational language*, we are generally referring to language that speaks of hopes, dreams, and affirmations ("You are the best!"). This kind of language—let's call it high motivation—has its role. But the message from Dweck and the hotbeds is clear: high motivation is not the kind of language that ignites people. What works is precisely the opposite: not reaching up but reaching down, speaking to the ground-level effort, affirming the struggle. Dweck's research shows that phrases like "Wow, you really tried hard," or "Good job, dude," motivate far better than what she calls empty praise.

From the myelin point of view, this conclusion makes sense. Praising effort works because it reflects biological reality. The truth is, skill circuits are not easy to build; deep practice requires serious effort and passionate work. The truth is, when you are starting out, you do not "play" tennis; you struggle and fight and pay attention and slowly get better. The truth is, we learn in staggering-baby steps. Effort-based language works because it speaks directly to the core of the learning experience, and when it comes to ignition, there's nothing more powerful.

"If I was a college, my success rate would be pretty good, *unowaime?*" Engblom said. "I mean, eighty or eighty-five percent of my guys end up successful businessmen, athletes, millionaires. You can't say that about Harvard."*

* Engblom would like to mention that he's free to talk to corporations or schools or anybody else to, "you know, advise them on personnel issues. I got a lot of thoughts on this stuff."

Chapter 7

How to Ignite a Hotbed

Education is not the filling of a pail,
but the lighting of a fire.
—W. B. Yeats

MIKE AND DAVE'S RIDICULOUS IDEA

Talent hotbeds like Curaçao, Russia, and South Korea were ignited by a lightning strike: a breakthrough star, a magical victory. No one could have predicted or planned them. A different kind of ignition occurs when there's no lightning strike and yet motivation and talent bloom anyway. This is the kind of ignition that relates more directly to our daily lives, and I found it happening most vividly in an unexpected place: a group of inner-city schools.

In the winter of 1993 Mike Feinberg and Dave Levin were not doing well. They were in their early twenties, roommates and second-year teachers in the Houston public school system. Both were members of Teach for America, a fledgling nonprofit group through which recent college graduates taught for two years in low-income schools. Feinberg and Levin's first year had been rocky (slashed tires, chaotic classes), their second year slightly worse. They'd tried to innovate but had found their efforts blocked by incompetent bureaucracy, unhelpful parents, misbehaving students, hidebound regulations, and the other blunt cogs of the most efficient frustration-machine ever invented: the American inner-city public school system. Levin had been asked not to return to his school; Feinberg, reaching an even deeper depth, found himself wishfully contemplating law school. So they spent their winter evenings sitting around their crummy Houston apartment engaging in the time-honored activity of twenty-somethings everywhere: bitching about work, drinking beer, and watching *Star Trek*. Their mindset was later summed up by Feinberg: "Life sucks, and then you die."

One night during that long winter, for reasons that remain mysterious (an inspiring speech they'd attended, they think, or maybe it was the beer), these two failed Gen X-ers suddenly had a perverse idea: they would stop fighting the system and start their own school. They put on a pot of coffee, set the stereo to play *Achtung Baby* by U2 on repeat, and by five A.M. they had printed a manifesto containing the four pillars of their creation: more classroom time, quality teachers, parental support, and administrative support. The caffeine must have kicked in, because the two baptized their project with a name that was as grandiose as anything Captain Kirk could dream up. They called it the Knowledge Is Power Program, or KIPP.

At any other moment in history, an idea as vague as KIPP, supported by little but inexperience, would have evaporated. But as it happened, Texas had recently passed laws funding charter schools, provided they achieved baseline educational standards. This resulted, a few months later, in a situation that would have previously been unthinkable: these two newbies and their coffee-stained manifesto would get their shot. Not a whole school (the board of education wasn't *that* crazy) but a single room in the corner of Garcia Elementary where Feinberg and Levin would be free to take the next inevitable step on their idealistic journey: fall on their faces.

The majority of charter schools are built on a foundation of educational theory, such as Waldorf, Montessori, or Piaget. Feinberg and Levin, short on time, instead followed the principles of Butch Cassidy: they stole. They located their district's best teachers and nabbed lesson plans, teaching techniques, management ideas, schedules, rules—everything. Feinberg and Levin would later be called "innovative," but at the time they were about as innovative as a shoplifter during a blackout. "We took every good idea that wasn't nailed down," Feinberg said. "We took everything but the kitchen sink, and then we went back and took the kitchen sink too."

From this pile of stolen parts they assembled an educational jalopy. It featured an engine of old-fashioned hard work (longer school days, shorter summer vacations, uniforms, a clear system of punishment and reward), encased in a skin of innovative techniques (times tables would be learned via rapping; kids would be given teachers' home phone numbers for homework questions). On the wall, Feinberg and Levin pasted a slogan pilfered from a renowned Los Angeles teacher named Rafe Esquith—"Work Hard, Be Nice"—and pointed their jalopy toward a distant goal: to do whatever it took to get the students into college.

"It was clear to us from the start that college is really the key to the whole thing," Feinberg said. "When you get out there in the public school system of big cities, you realize how screwed up it is—how the zipcode you're born in basically determines your chance of failing or succeeding. College is the door out."

That spring and summer Feinberg and Levin set about recruiting subjects for their experiment. After an intensive neighborhood campaign, they wound up with fifty students, most of whose parents were just as frustrated with the status quo as Feinberg and Levin were. When KIPP's first class walked into the tiny room for their first day, college seemed a long way off. The students ranked well below average in ability: only 53 percent had passed the state English and math tests the previous year. The room was overcrowded; their host school put up a steady resistance to their presence; the longer school days (seven-thirty A.M. to five P.M., plus classes every other Saturday, per the manifesto) put a strain on everyone.

But then something strange happened. It was impossible to put a finger on it, but at some point that autumn the jalopy coughed, sputtered, and started moving. To the amazement of everyone—not least Feinberg and Levin—the KIPP students lived up to their slogan: they were nice, and they worked hard. Extremely hard. At the end of the first year 90 percent of the students passed the state exams.

Encouraged, Feinberg and Levin kept going. For the first years they taught like nomads—Feinberg stayed in Houston while Levin relocated to the Bronx. They fought for space, taught in trailers, and cadged unused rooms. Each year they stole more good ideas and tossed out the ones that failed. And each year KIPP's test scores kept rising. By 1999 the KIPP academies in Houston and the Bronx were scoring higher on standardized tests than any other public schools in their respective districts. The jalopy wasn't just picking up speed; it was lapping the field.

Word spread. After a *60 Minutes* report, KIPP received a $15 million donation from Donald and Doris Fisher, founders of the Gap clothing store. Dozens, then hundreds of young teachers (many of them from the Teach for America program, which has subsequently become highly successful, placing 2,900 new teachers each year and attracting applications from 10 percent of Georgetown's, Yale's, and Harvard's 2008 graduating classes) signed on to start their own KIPP schools. By 2008 there were sixty-six KIPP schools from Los Angeles to New York, serving 16,000 students. Many KIPP schools now produce students who achieve some of the highest scores in their respective cities, and, most crucially, 80 percent of KIPP students go on to attend college. Feinberg and Levin still teach fifth graders in Houston and the Bronx, in addition to overseeing the KIPP schools in their areas and working on KIPP's national board of directors. Jason Snipes, a member of Harvard University's Council of Great City Schools, sums up their success in Andruw Jones terms: "KIPP is really knocking it out of the park."

One way to look at KIPP is as a unique tale of good-hearted underdogs who caught lightning in a bottle. If that were all it was, our interest in the story would end now. The other way to look at it, however, is as an example of pure ignition: the art and science of creating a talent hotbed from the ground up, without the assistance of a World Series homer or any other magical breakthrough. That's why it's useful to look under the hood of this remarkable jalopy to see what makes it go.

CURTAIN UP

At most schools the first day of a new academic year is likened to the first few strides of a marathon run, or perhaps the first skirmish of an insurgent war. At KIPP schools like KIPP Heartwood Academy in San Jose, California, however, the first day is like opening night for a Broadway play. There are scripts, timed entrances, and plotlines, a nervous audience, and, ten minutes before curtain, a backstage preshow huddle. At KIPP Heartwood that teachers' huddle takes place in an empty classroom a few steps from the outdoor courtyard where the students are beginning to assemble.

"Okay, people, let's be quick and sharp out there," says Sehba Ali, the school leader, to her staff of fifteen teachers. "We'll clap them in, do the welcome, the college talk, introduce each teacher, then do the 'be nice' talk at the end. Everybody got it?"

Sehba Ali is thirty-one years old and five feet tall. She is wearing a sleek beige pantsuit and softly clicking high heels, and she carries herself with a silken but unmistakable authority—a hybrid of Audrey Hepburn and Erwin Rommel. Ali has no earthly need to repeat this information: it's all neatly typed on the script for the day, which accounts for every event, transition, and activity. For the past few days, the staff has been reviewing the script in detail. They spent, for instance, a full hour discussing the correct body spacing and foot placement for KIPP fifth graders standing in a straight line. By now this day has been rehearsed and practiced "to a nit," as Ali puts it.

In the courtyard, milling in the early-morning sunshine, stand the 140 new KIPP students and their families. The kids are jumpy; the parents smother their own nervousness with reassuring smiles and hugs. They are mostly Hispanic, with a handful of Asians and African Americans; they come from San Jose's boundless sea of low-rent bungalows and government-subsidized apartments. Like many KIPP schools, this one began small, with Ali's door-to-door neighborhood campaign in 2004, as she asked parents about their experiences in the public school and inquired if they might be interested in an alternative. (Around the neighborhood Ali was known as "The Lady Who Asks a Lot of Questions.") The first year KIPP had 75 fifth graders; since then they've added 275 more students and three additional grade levels, and now they have a fast growing waiting list. All of which helps account for the atmosphere of poignant excitement here in the courtyard. The air is filled with a sense of irrevocable departure, as if the kids are boarding an ocean liner bound for a new world. While the vast majority of KIPP Heartwood students come from the local school district, not all of them do. Latha Narayannan had driven her son an hour from their home in Fremont, California. Narayannan, who had a well-paying job with an Internet consulting firm, said the public schools in her neighborhood were high-quality. She had come to KIPP, however, because she wanted to make 100 percent sure that her son, Ajiit, would go on to attend college. "I heard about what they do here," she said. "I said, I want this for my child."

At precisely eight A.M. Ali and the rest of the teachers walk to the courtyard. Ali claps five times. The other teachers join in, counting them out. The kids fall silent; the parents instinctively fall away.

"Good morning," Ali says loudly.

The kids murmur.

"GOOD MORNING," Ali repeats.

"Good morning," a few say.

Ali tilts her head, disappointed, expectant.

"GOOD MORNING," she tries again.

Another teacher, Lolita Jackson, offers the right response—"Good morning, Ms. Ali."

This time they get it. The next time Ali prompts them, the response comes in a chorus, "GOOD MORNING, MS. ALI."

Ali welcomes them, referring to each class by its new name. The fifth graders are the Class of 2015; the sixth are 2014; the number refers to the year in which they'll enter college. Ali then calls upon a group of returning students, distinctive in their white and green KIPP shirts, to model a line. They place their sneakers precisely along one of the colored stripes painted on the courtyard: eyes forward, hands down, neatly spaced.

"*This* is what a line at KIPP looks like," Ali says, as an assistant translates in Spanish. "DOES EVERYONE UNDERSTAND?"

"YES, MS. ALI," they say as one, catching on.

Each child is introduced by name, handed a large three-ring binder, and given a group-clap of praise, on the beat. Backpacks, water bottles, and coats are left with parents—they need nothing. KIPP teachers walk up and down the growing lines, making sure binders are held in the left hand (nice and flat, with spine down), that feet are straight, hands are extended, shirts tucked in. Urged to smile, none do. Ali walks the line. She stops at one boy and makes a twenty-degree correction in the angle at which he is holding his binder.

This is KIPP culture. It covers how to walk, how to talk (they work on the three-inch voice, the twelve-inch voice, and the room voice), how to sit at a desk (forward, upright, no pencil in hand), how to look at a teacher or classmate who's speaking (called *tracking:* head up, eyes on them, shoulders toward the speaker), and even how to negotiate the bathroom (use four or five sheets of toilet paper, one squirt of soap to wash hands). KIPP teachers plant trash around the school and see who picks it up, then celebrate that person in front of the group. They are constantly executing precise routines of clapping, chanting, and walking together. (Older students operate under more relaxed rules—they needn't walk in lines, for instance—but even those privileges are earned.)

"Every single detail matters," Feinberg says. "Everything they do is connected to everything else around them."

After forming lines, the new students are brought into a classroom, where they sit on the floor along taped lines. There are no desks because, the students are informed, they haven't earned them yet. The students open their binders to find several pages of math problems. This is "silent work time," a morning staple at KIPP. After half an hour of cathedral-like silence (the first few whispers and giggles are hushed by teachers; after that, the quiet takes hold), Ms. Ali strides to the front of the room and welcomes them again by their class names.

"Our goal—everyone tracking me now—as a team and family is that every single person in this room is going to COLLEGE."

Ali stops and lets the idea sink in. She repeats the phrase "going to college" with slow and reverent relish, the same way a priest might say "going to heaven." "Where are we going?" she asks.

"College" comes the tentative reply.

Hand cupped to her ear, Ali feigns deafness.

"COLLEGE!" they shout louder.

Ali smiles—a flash of happiness—then gets serious.

"I'm going to be straight with you. There are a lot of people who think you can't do it. Because your family doesn't have money. Because you're Latino or Vietnamese. But here at KIPP we believe in you. If you work hard and are nice, you *will* go to college and have a successful life. You will be extraordinary because here we work really, really hard, and that makes you smart.

"You WILL make mistakes. You WILL mess up. We will too. But you will all have beautiful behavior. Because everything here at KIPP is earned. EVERYTHING is earned. Everything is EARNED.

"You're on the floor. Are you uncomfortable? Do you wish you had desks? You will have to earn them. When you can track, when you clap together, when you can act like KIPP students, then you can have those desks."

Ali's dark brown eyes search the room, seeking connections. The students gaze back, nervous, excited, fully awake. To an outsider like me, the level of discipline seems over the top (which is why neighborhood smart alecks call it the Kids in Prison Program), but the results are clear: these kids are responding, engaging.

"We are watching you," Ali continues. "Everything here is a test. Everything here is earned. Is that clear?"

They nod.

"When I say *clear*, you say *crystal*," Ali says.

She looks around the room, her eyes glittering expectantly. She tries again: "Is that clear?"

One hundred and forty voices say, "CRYSTAL."

If we had to classify the primal cues the KIPP students received in those first few minutes, they would fall into three categories.

1. You belong to a group.
2. Your group is together in a strange and dangerous new world.
3. That new world is shaped like a mountain, with the paradise of college at the top.

These three signals might seem unique. But in fact they're identical to the primal cues that any young Brazilian soccer player or Russian tennis player might receive, if you replaced the word *college* with the words *being Ronaldinho/Kournikova*. Bereft of such naturally occurring aspirational figures, KIPP does the next best thing. It creates its own São Paolo, a signal-rich world so seamless that it creates new patterns of motivation and behavior—hence KIPP's Spielbergian insistence on timing, continuity, and plot. Like Frank Curiel Field in Curaçao, KIPP's physical environs radiate signals. Like a squadron of Tom Sawyers, KIPP's teachers fire cues rapidly and clearly. As Feinberg likes to say, "Everything is everything." This sounds like new-age palaver, but what he's really talking about is KIPP's insistence on environmental coherency: the way every element of this world, from the painted stripes on the floor to the eyes of the teacher, to the angle with which students carry their binders, sends clear, constant signals of belonging and identity: you are at KIPP, you are a KIPPster. Instead of "ready, set, go," they say "ready, set, KIPP." Students address each other as "teammates." KIPP teachers refer to this process only half-jokingly as "KIPP-nosis."

"I remember when I came to visit," said Michael Mann, who teaches social studies. "I thought it was way extreme. I thought it was ridiculous. I mean, who *cares* how they hold their binder? But I came to see that attention to detail is a big part of what makes someone academically successful. The rules are ways of getting them to practice being detailed and precise—and that's not something a lot of them have had any experience with."

KIPP teachers are not alone in their belief in this tactic. In 2005 psychologists Martin Seligman and Angela Duckworth studied several parameters of 164 eighth graders, including IQ, along with five tests that measured self-discipline. It turned out that self-discipline was twice as accurate as IQ in predicting the students' grade-point average.

"For every year [of their lives] up to now, [the students have] been acting in certain ways," Feinberg said. "The culture is an incredibly strong force, and the only way to reach them is to change the way they see themselves. It seems intense to somebody visiting, but that's what it takes."

One of the ways KIPP creates that change is through a technique it calls *stopping the school*. This is not fanciful language. When someone violates a significant rule, classes screech to a halt, and teachers and students hold a meeting to discuss what just happened and how to fix it.* A few weeks before I visited, the school had stopped because a sixth grader had teased another student, calling her an elephant. The previous stop had happened when a student rolled his eyes at a teacher. By most reasoning, stopping the school when a student teases or rolls their eyes is a gigantic waste of time. And yet it works. KIPP, like a giant Link trainer, creates an environment for deep-practicing good behavior. Stopping the school for an eye roll is not inefficient; on the contrary, KIPP has found that it's the most efficient way to establish

---

* Not surprisingly, from a deep-practice point of view at least, Toyota employs the same technique on its assembly lines, with great success (see page 210).

group priorities, locate errors, and build the behavioral circuits that KIPP desires.

As you can tell, KIPP's most important signal—its version of an Andruw Jones home run—is college. Or as it's invariably voiced at KIPP, *College!* College is the *spiritus sancti* that is invoked hundreds of times each day, not so much as a place as a glowing ideal. Each homeroom is named after the college the teacher attended: math classes are in Berkeley; social studies in USC; special education at Cornell Graduate School. KIPP teachers are skilled at slipping references to college into conversation, always with the presumption that all the students are destined for those golden shores. While I visited a social studies class, one student turned in her homework without her name on it. Her teacher's response was to stop the class. "You know how many papers your college professor is going to get?" the teacher asked, radiating incredulity. "You think he's going to take the time to figure out it's yours? Think about that." As English teacher Leslie Eichler said, "We say *college* as often as people in other schools say *um*." Even the lettering above the classroom mirrors inquires, "Where will YOU go to college?"

KIPP students start visiting colleges as soon as they're enrolled. KIPP Heartwood's fifth graders go to California schools like USC, Stanford, and UCLA, while seventh graders fly to the East Coast to walk the campuses of Yale, Columbia, and Brown, among others. While there, they meet with KIPP alumni who tell of their own journeys.

"Right now college is just a vague idea to them," Ali tells me later, gesturing at the new fifth graders. "But by the end of the fifth grade, after they make a visit, we overhear them talking about it among themselves, saying things like 'Yeah,

I like Berkeley, but I think I'm more of a Cal Poly person.' That's when we know it's clicking."

"When they get to KIPP, their lives are like a single dot on a map. You can't do anything with a dot," Feinberg said. "But when they connect that dot to another dot, to a college somewhere, then you get a connection. When they get back from those trips, they carry themselves differently."

This simple, powerful idea is made real in Lolita Jackson's math class. Jackson, who's in her late fifties, is a small woman who wears gigantic earrings and radiates galvanic discipline and enthusiasm. She spent the first twenty years of her career working in the local public school system, increasingly frustrated by its limitations. When KIPP Heartwood came along, however, she joined up and quickly rose to become one of its most effective teachers as well as its assistant principal. Ali regards Jackson's skills as near-magical. ("Ms. Jackson does things that nobody else can do," Ali says simply.) For instance, each year after orientation week is finished, Jackson begins her first math class by clicking off the lights and asking students to close their eyes. She slips a *Star Wars* soundtrack into the CD player and turns it up. As the triumphal music surges, Jackson strides around the room as if she were the captain of a rocket ship on countdown.

"You buckled up, KIPPsters?" she asks. "You ready? You strapped in good and tight? Because this is going to be a bumpy ride. It's going to be tough, and it's going to be hard, but it's also going to be great because we are going to work and learn some math, and we are going to college!"

The kids sit quietly, the music resounding in their heads.

"College," Jackson repeats, tasting the word. "Do you want to know the difference between a good life and a hard life? You want to know the difference between having the knowledge and power to get the things you want and not having that knowledge? Fasten your seat belts, because that's where you are going, starting right *now*."

Like Spartak, Meadowmount, and the other talent hotbeds, KIPP Heartwood is a bastion of deep practice. Jackson and her colleagues constantly remind KIPP students that their brains are muscles: the more they work them, the smarter they will get—and there's plenty of work to do. Two hours of homework a night is standard; worksheets number in the hundreds; the day is filled with stretches of intense, silent work. As Feinberg said, "Softer methods might work in other schools, but we literally don't have any hours to waste, much less days or weeks. Our kids arrive way behind; we need to get them up to speed and ahead. It's like the fourth quarter of a football game, we're down by a touchdown, and we've got to get downfield and score, now." The touchdowns are happening: in 2007, KIPP Heartwood students ranked in the top 3 percent of California public schools, according to the state's Standardized Testing and Reporting program.

What's striking in the end, however, is not how hard KIPP students work, but rather how swiftly and completely they take on the KIPP identity that provides the fuel for that hard work. On both of my visits I was approached by students who wanted to know how I was doing, if there was anything they might do for me, and of course where I went to college. Some of these exchanges felt a bit scripted (the overly firm handshakes, the fervently agreeable nodding, the geisha-level politeness), but beneath the artifice vibrated the sincere effort of someone stretching toward a new persona.

"I like it here a lot," said Daniel Magana, a crew-cut sixth grader. "There's no special treatment for anybody. At my old school they let me slide. I could do five out of ten things and nobody cared. Here I do ten out of ten."

Daniel, whose father is a construction worker, plans to be the first member of his family to attend college. He's not so sure which college yet. He's going to consider the California system—it's so much cheaper, you know—and he needs a pretty big school, one that offers a double major in his desired fields of laser surgery and creative writing. So he's thinking Berkeley. "But that could change," he said sagely. "We'll see."

When I asked Daniel to tell me what he was like back before he enrolled in KIPP, he looked gravely to the tile floor, as if peering into an ancient archaeological dig. "Different," he said finally. "I think I didn't really like school. It was boring. At my old school I used twenty-five percent of my brain, but here I use one hundred percent."

Ancient history didn't hold his interest long, however, and soon Daniel raced off on new tangents, inquiring about the ages of my kids and recommending books for them, asking about my travels, and then checking the clock and saying sorry, nice talking with you, but he'd better get to English class (handshake), good-bye, and I'm left standing with a question: Who, exactly, is this kid? How much of Daniel is Daniel, and how much is a result of his experience at KIPP?

There's no way to say whether Daniel Magana would have been an ambitious, considerate, high-achieving kid had he not attended KIPP. Perhaps he would have been the same; or perhaps, once he graduates from KIPP, he'll revert to old patterns. But as I watch him disappear into the crowd, I'm struck by how KIPP alters our instinctive notion of character. Usually, we think of character as deep and unchanging, an innate quality that flows outward, showing itself through behavior. KIPP shows that character might be more like a skill—ignited by certain signals, and honed through deep practice.

Seen this way, KIPP stands on a foundation of myelin. Every time a KIPP student imagines himself in college, a surge of energy is created, not unlike that created in South Korea when girls imagine themselves to be Se Ri Pak. Every time a KIPP student forces himself to obey one of these persnickety rules, a circuit is fired, insulated, and strengthened. (Impulse control, after all, is a circuit like any other.) Every time the entire school screeches to a halt to fix misbehavior, skills are being built as surely as they were when Clarissa did her start-stop attack on "Golden Wedding." No wonder Daniel Magana is such a polite, well-disciplined young man— he has been ignited to deep-practice those qualities.

"What we do here is like lighting a switch," Ali said. "It's extremely deliberate. It's not random; there's no chance involved. You have to stand behind what you do, to make sure every single detail is pushing the same way. Then it clicks. The kids get it, and when it starts, the rest of them get it, too. It's contagious."

3

Master Coaching

Chapter 8

The Talent Whisperers

It's not about recognizing talent, whatever the hell
that is. I've never tried to go out and find someone
who's talented. First you work on fundamentals,
and pretty soon you find out where things are going.
—*Robert Lansdorp, tennis coach of former world number-one players*
Pete Sampras, Tracy Austin, and Lindsay Davenport, all of whom
grew up within a few miles of each other in Los Angeles

THE ESP OF HANS JENSEN

In the early part of the twentieth century, American bank robbers weren't very skilled. Gangs like the Newton Brothers of Texas followed a simple and unvarying plan: they picked a bank, waited until nightfall, then blew open the vault with dynamite and/or nitroglycerine (which, in addition to being ticklish to handle, occasionally had the unfortunate side effect of setting the money on fire). This straightforward approach worked well for a time. But by the early 1920s the banks had caught up, introducing alarm systems and concrete-reinforced, blast-proof vaults. Gangs like the Newtons were stymied; bank authorities expected that a new era of safety and security had dawned.

It didn't dawn. The bank robbers simply became more skilled. These new thieves worked in daylight and operated with such clockwork professionalism that even the police were occasionally moved to admiration. It was as if bank robbers had suddenly evolved into a more talented species. They demonstrated their capabilities in downtown Denver on December 19, 1922, when a gang relieved the Federal Mint of $200,000 in ninety seconds flat, a feat that then ranked, on a per-second basis, among history's most lucrative bank heists.

This evolution could be traced to the man who led that Denver gang: Herman "The Baron" Lamm. Lamm was the originator and teacher of modern bank-robbing skill. Born in Germany around 1880, Lamm rose to become an officer in the Prussian Army. Expelled from the army (allegedly for cheating at cards), he emigrated to the United States, where he took up a semisuccessful career as a holdup man, robbing people and occasionally banks. In 1917, while serving a two-year stint in Utah State Prison, Lamm conceived of a new system of bank robbery, applying military principles to what had been an artless profession. His singular insight was that robbing banks was not about guts or guns; it was about technique.

Each bank job involved weeks of preparatory work. Lamm pioneered "casing," which meant visiting the bank, sketching blueprintlike maps, and occasionally posing as a journalist to get a look at the bank's interior operations. Lamm assigned each man on his team a well-defined role: lookout, lobby man, vault man, driver. He organized rehearsals, using warehouses to stand in for the bank. He insisted on unyielding obedience to the clock: when the allotted time expired, the gang would depart, whether or not they had the money. Lamm scouted the getaway route in different

weather conditions to gauge time; he taped maps to the dash-
board that were indexed to the tenth of a mile.

Lamm's system—dubbed the Baron Lamm Technique—
worked well. From 1919 to 1930 it brought Lamm hundreds of
thousands of dollars from banks around the country; after his
death it was taught to John Dillinger, among others.* Lamm's
system, still employed today, succeeded not only because of
its conceptual strength but also because Lamm was able to
communicate his ideas and translate them into the seamless
performance of an immensely difficult task. He was an inno-
vator who taught with discipline and exactitude. He inspired
through information. In short, Baron Lamm was a master
coach.

So far in this book we've talked about skill as a cellular
process that grows through deep practice. We've seen how ignition supplies the unconscious energy for that growth. Now
it's time to meet the rare people who have the uncanny knack
for combining those forces to grow talent in others.

Before we find out who the master coaches are, however, let's
find out who they aren't. When most of us think of a master
coach, we think of a Great Leader, a person of steadfast vision, battle-tested savvy, and commanding eloquence. Like a
ship's captain, or a preacher on the pulpit, their core ability
lies in knowing a special something that the rest of us don't,

---

* Lamm died in 1930 when he encountered a series of events so improbable that even he
could not have anticipated them. He was departing a bank in Clinton, Indiana, when the
getaway car blew a tire. Lamm and three members of his gang commandeered another
car, but it was equipped with a governor that prevented it from going faster than 35
mph. They commandeered a third, but it suffered a radiator leak. They commandeered
a fourth, but its tank contained only a gallon of gas. After a short chase, and the surren-
der of two gang members, the doubtlessly incredulous Lamm and his driver were shot
to death by police.

and sharing that special knowledge with us in a motivating way. In this way of thinking, the skills of legendary football coach Vince Lombardi are not appreciably different from those of General George Patton or Queen Elizabeth I. But when I visited the talent hotbeds, I didn't find many Lombardis or Pattons, or Queen Elizabeths for that matter.

Instead, the teachers and coaches I met were quiet, even reserved. They were mostly older; many had been teaching thirty or forty years. They possessed the same sort of gaze: steady, deep, unblinking. They listened far more than they talked. They seemed allergic to giving pep talks or inspiring speeches; they spent most of their time offering small, targeted, highly specific adjustments. They had an extraordinary sensitivity to the person they were teaching, customizing each message to each student's personality. After meeting a dozen of these people, I started to suspect that they were all secretly related. They were talent whisperers. They were people like Hans Jensen.

Hans Jensen is a cello teacher who lives in Chicago. I met him at Meadowmount Music School, that remote haven of classical talent in the Adirondacks we visited earlier in the book. I had never heard of Jensen, but here, even amidst an all-star faculty, he was regarded as special. During my first morning at Meadowmount two students mentioned how their families had relocated to Chicago so they could take lessons from Jensen. Melissa Kraut, who teaches at the Cleveland Institute of Music, simply described him as "the most brilliant cello teacher on the planet."

Jensen turned out to be a rangy, ebullient fiftyish Dane with large round glasses, from behind which he regarded the world with the voracious gaze of a scuba diver. When I found him in one of Meadowmount's practice cabins, that gaze was aimed at eighteen-year-old Sang Yhee, who was playing a Dvořák concerto. To my ear, Sang's playing was miraculous: fast, clean, note-perfect. But Jensen was not satisfied. He stood a few inches away as the student played, waving his arms and talking to Sang in his thick Danish accent. It looked as if Jensen were performing some kind of exorcism.

"Now! Now!" he shouted. "There is only now! You gotta go *wahhhh*, like a turbine. You gotta do it, man, and you gotta do it now."

Sang played furiously, his hand flashing up and down the neck of the cello.

Jensen leaned in closer. "I see it in your eyes—you say, 'Oh crap, I have to do it.' So don't think [pronounced *sink* in Jensen's accent]. Do it! NOW!"

Sang closed his eyes and played.

"Yah! Yah!" Jensen shouted. "GO! GO!"

Sang ended the piece and leaned back woozily, as if he had just stepped off a carnival ride.

"There," Jensen said. "That is where you have to go with this."

Sang thanked Jensen, packed up his cello, and departed as Whitney Delphos, the next student, stepped forward. Delphos was twenty years old, from Houston, and wore a pink Lacoste shirt with the collar turned up. She had arrived in time to see the end of Sang's lesson and now took her seat, grasping the neck of her instrument, sweating lightly.

Jensen put her at ease, leaning back in his chair, smiling broadly. "Howdy," he said disarmingly.

Delphos smiled and seemed to relax a little. Jensen asked her to play and he listened quietly as she dove into a Bach concerto. Delphos was shakier than Sang. She smudged a few notes, lost the rhythm of a fast passage, and generally seemed to be wrestling with the instrument. She glanced warily at Jensen as she played, expecting him to launch into another arm-waving, shouting exhibition as he had with Sang.

But Jensen didn't. After thirty seconds he placed a gentle hand on her bow, stilling it. He leaned in, as if he were about to whisper a state secret.

"You must sink it," he said.

"Sink it?" Delphos was mystified.

Jensen tapped his bald head, and she understood. *"Sink,"* he repeated. "Sink the whole piece. When you sink it, it is ten times better. People practice too much, moving the bow. You must practice up here!" He pointed again to his head. "You must sink! This is the vitamin. It doesn't taste good. But it's good for you."

Delphos set down her bow, closed her eyes, and as instructed, imagined her way through sections of her concerto. When she was finished, her eyes open again, Jensen said, "You used vibrato when you imagined playing that last section, didn't you?"

Delphos's jaw dropped. "How did you know?"

Jensen smiled. "I sometimes freak people out," he said. "They sink I have ESP."

Jensen has a long list of professional qualifications. He studied at Juilliard with renowned teachers Leonard Rose and Channing Robbins; he's soloed with the Copenhagen Symphony and won the Artist International Competition. His knowledge of classical cello music is second to none. But what we're seeing here has nothing to do with Jensen's qualifications and everything to do with his mysterious ESP—specifically, his skill at sensing the student's needs and instantly producing the right signal to meet those needs.

Jensen did not know Sang and Delphos before they stepped into the room. He didn't need to. The examination, diagnosis, and prescription all happened within seconds. Sang needed more emotion, so Jensen turned into a hepped-up cheerleader; Delphos needed a learning strategy, so Jensen turned into a Zen master. He didn't only tell them what to do: he *became* what they should do, communicating the goal with gesture, tone, rhythm, and gaze. The signals were targeted, concise, unmissable, and accurate.

After Jensen was finished teaching Sang and Delphos, I asked him for his professional opinion of the two students. Which was more talented? Which had more potential? Jensen seemed to struggle with the question, which surprised me. (Sang seemed better than Delphos, by a decent margin.) But the planet's best cello teacher didn't see things the same way I did.

"It's difficult to say," Jensen said evenly. "When I teach, I give everyone everything. What happens after that, who can know?"

This sentiment—even-keeled, prudent, unromantic—had a familiar ring. Many of the talent whisperers reminded me of my relatives in Illinois farming towns, who were tough, unsurprisable, and circumspect. They could talk for hours about the tiniest details of seeds or fertilizers, but when it came to the larger questions—the quality of the upcoming harvest, the playoff chances of their beloved St. Louis Cardinals baseball team—they shrugged. *Who can know?*

Master coaches aren't like heads of state. They aren't like captains who steer us across the unmarked sea, or preachers on a pulpit, ringing out the good news. Their personality—their core skill circuit—is to be more like farmers: careful, deliberate cultivators of myelin, like Hans Jensen. They're down-to-earth and disciplined. They possess vast, deep frameworks of knowledge, which they apply to the steady, incremental work of growing skill circuits, which they ultimately don't control. Jensen couldn't answer my question because at its heart the question didn't make sense. Is it possible to look at two seedlings and tell which will grow taller? The only answer is *It's early and they're both growing*.

THE WIZARD'S SECRET

In 1970 two educational psychologists named Ron Gallimore and Roland Tharp were given a dream opportunity: to set up, from scratch, an experimental reading program at a laboratory school in a poor neighborhood in Honolulu. The project, which was funded by a Hawaiian educational foundation, involved 120 K-3 students and was dubbed the Kamehameha Early Education Project, or KEEP. Starting in 1972, when the school's doors opened, Gallimore and Tharp applied the most cutting-edge pedagogical theories of the day, many of which had to do with teacher strategies to increase the percentage of "on task" time. Gallimore and Tharp were innovative, hardworking, and determined. They also weren't very successful. For the first two years, reading achievement at KEEP remained low. By the summer of 1974, Gallimore recalled, "we were starting to seriously question our methodology."

That summer happened to find both Gallimore and Tharp at UCLA, where they taught a few classes and puzzled over their stalled-out project. One afternoon while shooting baskets in Gallimore's backyard, Gallimore had an idea: they would perform a detailed, up-close case study of the greatest teacher they could find and use the results to help them at

KEEP. Both men instantly thought of the same teacher, who happened to be right on UCLA's campus. Yet they hesitated. This particular teacher was so brilliant and acclaimed that to ask him to be a lab rat in a study seemed unthinkable, if not insolent. But Gallimore and Tharp, with nothing to lose, decided to write the famous teacher anyway. They mailed their request to his office in Pauley Pavilion, addressed to Mr. John Wooden, head basketball coach.

To describe John Wooden as a good basketball coach is like describing Abraham Lincoln as a solid congressman. The Wizard of Westwood, as Wooden was known, was a former English teacher from small-town Indiana who quoted Wordsworth and lived Christian values of discipline, morality, and teamwork. He had led UCLA to nine national championships in the previous ten years. His team had recently concluded an eighty-eight-game undefeated stretch that had lasted for nearly three years, one of the many historic feats that would later lead ESPN to name Wooden the greatest coach of all time in any sport. As Gallimore and Tharp were well aware, Wooden had no earthly reason to submit himself to the prying of a couple of nosy scientists. So they were more than a little surprised when Wooden's answer arrived: *yes.*

A few weeks later Gallimore and Tharp settled eagerly into courtside seats at Pauley Pavilion to watch Wooden coach the season's first practice. As fans of the team as well as former athletes themselves, they knew what to expect: chalk talks, inspiring speeches, punishment laps for slackers, praise for hard workers.

Then practice began.

Wooden didn't give speeches. He didn't do chalk talks. He didn't dole out punishment laps or praise. In all, he didn't sound or act like any coach they'd ever encountered.

"We thought we knew what coaching was," Gallimore said. "Our expectations were completely wrong. Completely. All the stuff I'd associated with coaching—there was none of it."

Wooden ran an intense whirligig of five- to fifteen-minute drills, issuing a rapid-fire stream of words all the while. The interesting part was the content of those words. As their subsequent article, "Basketball's John Wooden: What a Coach Can Teach a Teacher," put it, Wooden's "teaching utterances or comments were short, punctuated, and numerous. There were *no* lectures, *no* extended harangues...he rarely spoke longer than twenty seconds."

Here are some of Wooden's more long-winded "speeches":

"Take the ball softly; you're receiving a pass, not intercepting it."

"Do some dribbling between shots."

"Crisp passes, really snap them. Good, Richard—that's just what I want."

"Hard, driving, quick steps."

Gallimore and Tharp were confused. They'd expected to find a basketball Moses intoning sermons from the mount, yet this man resembled a busy telegraph operator. They felt slightly deflated. *This* was great coaching?

Gallimore and Tharp kept attending practices. As weeks and months went by, an ember of insight began to glow. It came partly from watching the team improve, rising from third in the conference at midseason to winning its tenth national championship. But it came mostly from the data they collected in their notebooks. Gallimore and Tharp recorded and coded 2,326 discrete acts of teaching. Of them, a mere 6.9 percent were compliments. Only 6.6 percent were expressions of displeasure. But 75 percent were pure information:

what to do, how to do it, when to intensify an activity. One of Wooden's most frequent forms of teaching was a three-part instruction where he modeled the right way to do something, showed the incorrect way, and then remodeled the right way, a sequence that appeared in Gallimore and Tharp's notes as M+, M-, M+; it happened so often they named it a "Wooden." As Gallimore and Tharp wrote, Wooden's "demonstrations rarely take longer than three seconds, but are of such clarity that they leave an image in memory much like a textbook sketch."

The information didn't slow down the practice; to the contrary, Wooden combined it with something he called "mental and emotional conditioning," which basically amounted to everyone running harder than they did in games, all the time. As former player Bill Walton said, "Practices at UCLA were nonstop, electric, supercharged, intense, demanding." While Wooden's practices looked natural and unplanned, in fact they were anything but. The coach would spend two hours each morning with his assistants planning that day's practice, then write out the minute-by-minute schedule on three-by-five cards. He kept cards from year to year, so he could compare and adjust. No detail was too small to be considered. (Wooden famously began each year by showing players how to put on their socks, to minimize the chance of blisters.) What looked like a flowing, improvised series of drills was in fact as well structured as a libretto. What looked like Wooden shooting from the hip was in fact closer to planned talking points.

As Gallimore and Tharp wrote, Wooden "made decisions 'on the fly' at a pace equal to his players, in response to the details of his players' actions. Yet his teaching was in no sense ad hoc. Down to the specific words he used, his planning included specific goals both for the team and for individuals. Thus, he could pack into a practice a rich basketball curriculum and deliver information at precisely the moments it would help his students learn the most."

Gradually a picture came into focus: what made Wooden a great coach wasn't praise, wasn't denunciation, and certainly wasn't pep talks. His skill resided in the Gatling-gun rattle of targeted information he fired at his players. *This, not that. Here, not there.* His words and gestures served as short, sharp impulses that showed his players the correct way to do something. He was seeing and fixing errors. He was honing circuits. He was a virtuoso of deep practice, a one-man Link trainer.

Wooden may not have known about myelin, but like all master coaches, he had a deep understanding of how it worked. He taught in chunks, using what he called the "whole-part method"—he would teach players an entire move, then break it down to work on its elemental actions. He formulated laws of learning (which might be retitled laws of myelin): explanation, demonstration, imitation, correction, and repetition. "Don't look for the big, quick improvement. Seek the small improvement one day at a time. That's the only way it happens—and when it happens, it lasts," he wrote in *The Wisdom of Wooden.* "The importance of repetition until automaticity cannot be overstated," he said in *You Haven't Taught Until They Have Learned,* authored by Gallimore and former Wooden player Swen Nater. "Repetition is the key to learning."

Most people regard Wooden's success as a product of his humble, thoughtful, inspiring character. But Gallimore and Tharp showed that his success was a result less of his character than of his error-centered, well-planned, information-rich practices. In fact, it was Wooden's commitment to this method of learning that led him to agree to participate in Gallimore and Tharp's experiment in the first place. As Wooden later explained, he had hoped to use the experience to improve shortcomings in his coaching. The wizard's secret, it turned out, was the same secret that the Renaissance artists and the Z-Boys discovered: the deeper you practice, the better you get.

Gallimore and Tharp returned to KEEP that fall and began to apply what they'd learned, placing a new focus on lesson planning and information-oriented teaching. They combined praise with "Woodens"; they demonstrated and explained; they spoke in short, imperative bursts. (They also added other new research, including a mix of cultural-based approaches.) "We refocused our work," Gallimore said. "We started approaching the school with the idea of, what would John Wooden do?"

Slowly, steadily, KEEP began to take off. Reading scores rose, comprehension improved, and the school, which had previously lagged far behind national averages in standardized test scores, was soon exceeding them by a healthy margin. In 1993 Gallimore and Tharp's KEEP project received the Grawemeyer Award, one of education's highest honors; their success was chronicled in their book, *Rousing Minds to Life*. "It's not so simple as to say John Wooden made the school work—there were lots of dimensions to this," Gallimore said. "But he does deserve a lot of the credit."

Even as we point out Wooden's coaching brilliance, however, it's important to note that he was hardly operating under average circumstances. His players arrived at UCLA with high degrees of skill and motivation; he had vast resources on which to draw. But what about coaches and teachers who live in the normal world? What kind of coaching works best in situations where students are starting out, where they haven't been selected for any special ability, where the circuitry doesn't yet exist? Or to put the question in terms that matter around our house, what makes for a good piano teacher?

COACHING LOVE

It's the most basic common sense: if you want to start a child in a new skill, you should search out the best-trained, most John Wooden–like teacher possible. Right?

Not necessarily. In the early 1980s a University of Chicago team of researchers led by Dr. Benjamin Bloom undertook a study of 120 world-class pianists, swimmers, tennis champions, mathematicians, neurologists, and sculptors. Bloom's team examined each along a range of dimensions, among which was their initial education in their chosen field. They discovered a surprising fact: many world-class talents, particularly in piano, swimming, and tennis, start out with seemingly average teachers.

For instance, Bloom's researchers asked the piano virtuosos to rate their first teacher as "very good" (defined as a highly regarded professional instructor with extensive training), "better than average" (a teacher with good training and more musical knowledge than a local neighborhood teacher), or "average" (a nonprofessional neighborhood teacher). Of the twenty-one internationally accomplished pianists in the study, only two had a first teacher who qualified as "very good." The majority had teachers who qualified as "average"

(62 percent) or "better than average" (24 percent). The pattern held in swimming and tennis. (The neurologists and mathematicians typically received their first training in school, which wasn't subject to the same variable of teacher choice, while the sculptors had not been guided by early instruction of any kind.) One might suspect that the average teacher was quickly replaced with someone more skilled, but that didn't seem to be the case. Bloom's pianists, for instance, had typically stayed with the first teacher for five or six years. From a scientific perspective, it was as if the researchers had traced the lineage of the world's most beautiful swans back to a scruffy flock of barnyard chickens. As the study concisely put it, "The initial teachers were largely determined by the chances of proximity and availability."

Chance? But aren't Wooden, Jensen, Preobrazhenskaya, and the other talent whisperers successful because their skills represent the precise opposite of chance? At first glance Bloom's study would seem to suggest that topflight talent is an innate genetic gift that transcends teaching. But perhaps something else is going on here.

As it happens, the town in which our family lives (population 5,000) is a bit of a musical hotbed. (Long winters don't hurt.) There are several topflight teachers with impressive degrees from top institutions, and a spanking-new music school. But when my wife and I decided to start our kids at piano lessons, we were directed toward someone we didn't expect: a little old lady who taught in a rickety house built around a trailer that stands next to a creek. Her name is Mary Epperson.

Mary Epperson is eighty-six years old and four feet six inches tall. She has thick white hair and keen dark eyes that seem custom-built to express curiosity and wonderment. Her voice is musical, able to stretch single words into brief songs of delight or conspiratorial whispers. She does not engage in small talk but rather holds previous conversations in her mind like so many threads, which she operates with sharp tugs. She begins most conversations with the phrase "Now tell me."

If you are a child visiting Miss Mary for a lesson, this is what happens. First, she is extremely pleased to see you; she lights up like a Christmas tree. You talk awhile about what's happening in your life and hers. She remembers all of it, of course: the camping trip, the English test, the new bike. She nods gravely at the serious points, laughs at the funny ones. She regards children as miniature adults and doesn't shy away from pointed truths. (Once Miss Mary asked my father if he ever played an instrument. He said he had tried piano but didn't have the knack. "Didn't have the patience, you mean," Miss Mary replied kindly but firmly.)

The lesson begins. By most measures, it's the usual routine. Songs are played, mistakes are made, improvements are suggested, stickers are pasted to tops of pages. But on a deeper level something entirely different is happening. Each interaction vibrates with Miss Mary's interest and emotion. To have better hand position is to earn a thrilling jolt of praise. To play something incorrectly brings a regretful "I'm sorry" and a request to please play it again. (And again. And perhaps again.) To play something properly brings a warm gust of joy. When it's over, there's a foil-wrapped chocolate, then you bow and say, "Thank you for teaching," and Miss Mary bows and solemnly replies, "Thank you for learning."

I thought of Miss Mary when I read the descriptions of the so-called average first piano teachers in Bloom's study.

She was really great with young kids.

She was very kindly, very nice.

She liked young people, and she was very nice, and he liked her.

He was very good with kids, liked kids instinctively and had a good rapport.

He was enormously patient and not very pushy.

She carried a big basket of Hershey bars and gold stars for the music and I was crazy about this lady.

It was an event for me to go to my lessons.

These people are not average teachers; neither is Mary Epperson. As Bloom and his researchers realized, they are merely disguised as average because their crucial skill does not show up on conventional measures of teaching ability. They succeed because they are tapping into the second element of the talent code: ignition. They are creating and sustaining motivation; they are teaching love. As Bloom's study summed up, "The effect of this first phase of learning seemed to be to get the learner involved, captivated, hooked, and to get the learner to need and want more information and expertise."

It is not easy to love playing the piano. It has lots of keys, and a child has lots of fingers, and there are an infinite number of mistakes that can be made. Yet certain teachers have the rare ability to make it desirable and fun. As Bloom's study put it, "Perhaps the major quality of these teachers was that they made the initial learning very pleasant and rewarding. Much of the introduction to the field was as playful activity, and the learning at the beginning of this stage was much like a game. These teachers gave much positive reinforcement and only rarely were critical of the child. However, they did set standards and expected the child to make progress, although this was largely done with approval and praise."

If Gallimore and Tharp were to conduct a study inside Miss Mary's tiny studio, they would find a stream of cues rich enough to rival those given on the Pauley Pavilion basketball court. This is not an accident. John Wooden uses the deep-practice part of the talent mechanism, speaking the language of information and correction, honing circuitry. Miss Mary, on the other hand, deals in matters of ignition, using emotional triggers to fill fuel tanks with love and motivation. They succeed because building myelin circuits requires both deep practice and ignition; they succeed because they are mirrors of the talent code itself.

Yet while myelin may be counted in wraps and hours, Wooden and Miss Mary also show us that master coaching is something more evanescent: more art than science. It exists in the space between two people, in the warm, messy game of language, gesture, and expression. To better understand how this process works, let's pull back and take a broader look at the shared characteristics of master coaches.

Chapter 9

The Teaching Circuit: A Blueprint

A teacher affects eternity; he can never
tell where his influence stops.
—Henry Brooks Adams

THE FOUR VIRTUES OF MASTER COACHES

Great teaching is a skill like any other. It only looks like magic; in fact, it is a combination of skills—a set of myelinated circuits built through deep practice. Ron Gallimore, who is now a distinguished professor emeritus at UCLA, has a good way of describing the skill. "Great teachers focus on what the student is saying or doing," he says, "and are able, by being so focused and by their deep knowledge of the subject matter, to see and recognize the inarticulate stumbling, fumbling effort of the student who's reaching toward mastery, and then connect to them with a targeted message."

The key words of this sentence are *knowledge, recognize,* and *connect.* What Gallimore is saying, and what Jensen, Wooden, and Miss Mary are showing, links back to our thesis: *Skill is insulation that wraps neural circuits and grows according to certain signals*. In the most literal sense, master coaches are the human delivery system for the signals that fuel and direct the growth of a given skill circuit, telling it with great clarity to fire *here* and *not here*. Coaching is a long, intimate conversation, a series of signals and responses that move toward a shared goal. A coach's true skill consists not in some universally applicable wisdom that he can communicate to all, but rather in the supple ability to locate the sweet spot on the edge of each individual student's ability, and to send the right signals to help the student reach toward the right goal, over and over. As with any complex skill, it's really a combination of several different qualities—what I have called "the four virtues."

THE MATRIX: THE FIRST VIRTUE

The coaches and teachers I met at the talent hotbeds were mostly older. More than half were in their sixties or seventies. All had spent decades, usually several, intensively learning how to coach. This is not a coincidence; in fact, it's a prerequisite, because it builds the neural superstructure that is the most essential part of their skills—their matrix.

Matrix is Gallimore's word for the vast grid of task-specific knowledge that distinguishes the best teachers and allows them to creatively and effectively respond to a student's efforts. Gallimore explains it this way: "A great teacher has the capacity to always take it deeper, to see the learning the student is capable of and to go there. It keeps going deeper and deeper because the teacher can think about the material in so many different ways, and because there's an endless number of connections they can make." Or as I would put it: years of work go into myelinating a master coach's circuitry, which is a mysterious amalgam of technical knowledge, strategy, experience, and practiced instinct ready to be put to instant use to locate and understand where the students are and where they need to go. In short, the matrix is a master coach's killer application.

We'll see how the matrix functions in a moment; for now the point is that people are not born with this depth of knowledge. It's something they grow, over time, through the same combination of ignition and deep practice as any other skill.* One does not become a master coach by accident. Many of the coaches I met shared a similar biographical arc: they had once been promising talents in their respective fields but failed and tried to figure out why. A good example is Louisiana-born Linda Septien, who eventually founded the Septien Vocal Studio in Dallas, Texas.

Septien is a tanned, youthful fifty-four-year-old who tends toward skin-tight tracksuits and metallic sneakers, and who possesses a natural exuberance that allows her to move past obstacles that would discourage most people. This exuberance shows itself in the way she talks (quickly, candidly, italicizing key words) and drives her BMW (only seventeen speeding tickets last year, she informs me) but also in her approach to the ups and downs of life. During our first conversation at her studio, she mentioned that her house had caught fire last year. How big a fire? I asked.

---

* As Anders Ericsson would remind us, reaching world-class status requires ten thousand hours of deep practice. So why did the master coaches tend to be older? Perhaps it was just chance, or perhaps it reflected social forces (after all, most children don't grow up wanting to become a coach in the same way they grow up wanting to become Tiger Woods). Or perhaps it illustrates a unique double requirement that coaches not only grow proficient in their chosen field but also learn how to teach it effectively.

"I wasn't there, but my neighbors said there were some *pret-ty* big explosions when the boat blew up," she said. "It took six fire engines to put it out. I lost *everything*—my piano, passport, clothing, photos, toothbrush, all burned up. My cockatoo Cleo got singed, but she made it. I didn't mind losing my stuff, but I minded losing the time—*that's* what's precious to me. I've had to move like six times in the last year while we built a new place, so that isn't any fun. But you know what?" Septien gave me a frank, dazzling smile. "I like the new house better. I really do."

Septien has had some practice rebuilding. In her early twenties she had a successful opera-singing career (performing with the New Orleans Symphony Orchestra) and a marriage to a famous football player, Dallas Cowboys placekicker Rafael Septien. But when she was in her late twenties, her opera career stalled out, and her marriage did likewise. In 1984, pregnant with her first child, on the verge of separating from her husband, she went to Nashville with the idea of making a transition to popular music and recording a Christian album. She auditioned with a team of record producers, singing "I'm a Miracle, Lord." The audition went well, or so she thought.

"I sang *beautifully;* I hit every note," she remembered. "And when it was finished, the producers sat there silently. I thought, 'I've stunned them. They know I'm great.'"

Septien smiled ruefully. "Then they told me the truth: I was *terrible*. Awful. They didn't care about notes, they cared about feeling, and I sang with no feeling, no passion, no story. I was a classical singer. I had *no* idea how to sell a song.

"I can't tell you how much this bothered me. I thought I was really, really good, really talented, and here were some guys who said flat out that I sucked—and they were right, I did suck. It made me really mad, and it also made me really curious. I wanted to figure out how to do this."

Septien spent the next few months taking care of her new baby and studying big pop and rock acts: Tom Jones, the Rolling Stones, U2. She studied the way they sang, moved, and spoke. She took notes, scribbling on napkins and programs, tucking her findings into large three-ring binders. Septien approached pop music like a medical student, systematically dissecting its various systems. How did Tom Jones manage his breathing in "Delilah"? How did Bono use movement to convey emotion in his songs? What made Willie Nelson's minimalist vocals so compelling? She watched audiences as much as artists, "to see what really turned them on."

Despite all this work Septien's singing career failed to lift off over the next few years. She made ends meet by selling real estate, working as a spokesperson, modeling, and on occasion teaching classical voice lessons out of her home. "It wasn't like I was a good teacher," she said. "I was the only ad for voice in the Dallas Yellow Pages." When youthful acts like Debbie Gibson and Tiffany succeeded in the early 1990s, Septien saw a growing trickle of kids who wanted to be pop stars. "I said, why not? I knew pop music. I just had to figure out how to teach it."

At first Septien taught pop the same way she'd learned classical, by teaching students to follow universal principles of technique. But that didn't work. "Really quickly I switched and became more artist-focused," she said. "I realized my job was to find out what worked for somebody and connect it to what worked in pop music. There was no system for doing that, so I had to invent my own."

Septien dug into her binders and, over the next few years, created a curriculum that applied the rigor and structure of classical training to the world of pop. She mined Whitney Houston vocals for scale exercises. She developed programs for diaphragm exercises, ear training, and scat singing. Like Feinberg and Levin at KIPP, she was constantly experimenting with new approaches, discarding, trying again. She made performing a central element, arranging gigs for her students at malls, schools, and rodeos. She required students to write their own songs, importing professional songwriters to teach them how. Over the years the matrix of her knowledge expanded. That expansion accelerated in 1991, when an eleven-year-old named Jessica Simpson showed up at Septien's studio for a lesson.

"She sang 'Amazing Grace,'" Septien recalled. "Jessica had an infectious personality—real sweet, but she was painfully shy on stage. Plus, her voice needed a *lot* of work. It was beautiful, but it was churchy, which made sense because her dad was a minister. She had a big vibrato." Septien demonstrates, filling her office with pulsating sound. "You can't sing pop music with a vibrato. You ever seen a pair of vocal cords? They're pink and shaped like a V—they're muscles, basically. The vibrato meant that Jessica wasn't controlling her cords properly, so we had to work at tightening them up, like you would a guitar string.

"The other thing with Jessica was that she had no feel, no expression, no connection to the emotion of the music, the same as I was when I started out. So we had to work a lot on that, on gestures, movement, connection to the audience, which is a whole skill in itself. The audience is like a big animal out there; you've got to learn to control it, connect to it, and make it breathe hard for more. Your voice can be incredible, but if you can't connect, it doesn't matter. But Jessica was a hard, hard worker. She really dove in."

It took two years to fix the vibrato, and a few more to learn stagecraft. By the time she was sixteen, after five years of working with Septien, Simpson had a record deal; three years later she had a 3.5 million–selling album and a platinum single, "I Wanna Love You Forever." Simpson was hailed as an overnight success, a term that continues to entertain Septien.

"Everybody said Jessica was a Texas girl who'd been singing in her church choir. That's ridiculous—that girl *worked* to become the singer she was. They said [*American Idol* winner] Kelly Clarkson was a waitress, like she never sang before. Waitress? Excuse me? Kelly Clarkson was a *singer*—we all knew Kelly Clarkson. She had training, and she worked her tail off like anybody else does. She didn't come from nowhere any more than Jessica came from nowhere. It's not magic, you know."

After Simpson, one thing led to another. Septien briefly worked with a rising Houston-area singer named Beyoncé Knowles, then used her ever-growing skills to develop and launch Ryan Cabrera, Demi Lovato, and several future *American Idol* finalists; her small studio became known as a star factory. On the day I was there, I heard singers from *High School Musical* and *Barney and Friends*, and a half-dozen pint-size Christina Aguileras. Septien was embarking on a roadshow for investors, seeking $100 million to expand the school to what her financial adviser called "the Gap of music schools." More important, her matrix is now complete. As Septien puts it, "Someone can walk in that door, and I know I can figure them out in twenty seconds."

"There's nothing she hasn't considered, nothing you can

stump her with," says Sarah Alexander, an ex-lawyer-turned-recording-artist who's worked with Septien. "She has the cognitive understanding of what my vocal cords are doing at any moment and exactly how they could be better. She always had an explanation that made the problem surmountable. Linda takes good care of the small steps."

"People see all the glitter and stage stuff, and they forget that vocal cords are just muscles," Septien said. "*They . . . are . . . just . . . muscles*. What I do for myself as a teacher is no different from what I ask my students to do. I know what I'm doing because I put a lot of work into it. I'm no different from them. If you spend years and years trying hard to do something, you'd *better* get better at it. How dumb would I have to be if I didn't?"

PERCEPTIVENESS: THE SECOND VIRTUE

The eyes are the giveaway. They are usually sharp and warm and are deployed in long, unblinking gazes. Several master coaches told me that they trained their eyes to be like cameras, and they share that same Panavision quality. Though the gaze can be friendly, it's not chiefly about friendship. It's about information. It's about figuring you out.

When Gallimore and Tharp studied John Wooden in 1974, they were surprised to find that he distributed praise and criticism unevenly. Which is to say, certain players got a lot of praise; others got a lot of criticism. What's more, he was open about this. During the team's preseason meeting each year, Wooden would say, "I am not going to treat you players all the same. Giving you the same treatment doesn't make sense, because you're all different. The good Lord, in his infinite wisdom, did not make us all the same. Goodness gracious, if he had, this would be a boring world, don't you think? You are different from each other in height, weight, background, intelligence, talent, and many other ways. For that reason, each one of you deserves individual treatment that is best for you. I will decide what that treatment will be."

Almost all the master coaches I met followed Wooden's rule. They wanted to know about each student so they could customize their communications to fit the larger patterns in a student's life. Football coach Tom Martinez, whom we'll meet later, has a vivid metaphor for this process. "The way I look at it, everybody's life is a bowl of whipped cream and shit, and my job is to even things out," he said. "If a kid's got a lot of shit in his life, I'm going to stir in some whipped cream. If a kid's life is pure whipped cream, then I'm going to stir in some shit."

On the macro level, the coaches I met approached new students with the curiosity of an investigative reporter. They sought out details of their personal lives, finding out about family, income, relationships, motivation. And on the micro level, they constantly monitored the student's reaction to their coaching, checking whether their message was being absorbed. This led to a telltale rhythm of speech. The coach would deliver a chunk of information, then pause, hawkeyeing the listener as if watching the needle of a Geiger counter. As Septien put it, "I'm always checking, because I need to know when they don't know."

"They are listening on many levels," Gallimore said. "They are able to use their words and behaviors as an instrument to move the student forward."

THE GPS REFLEX: THE THIRD VIRTUE

"You gotta give them a lot of information," said Robert Lansdorp, the tennis coach. "You gotta shock 'em, then shock 'em some more."

Shock is an appropriate word. Most master coaches delivered their information to their students in a series of short, vivid, high-definition bursts. They never began sentences with "Please, would you" or "Do you think" or "What about"; instead they spoke in short imperatives. "Now do X" was the most common construction; the "you will" was implied. The directions weren't dictatorial in tone (usually) but were delivered in a way that sounded clinical and urgent, as if they were being emitted by a particularly compelling GPS unit navigating through a maze of city streets: *turn left, turn right, go straight, arrival complete.*

For example, here is a transcript of three minutes of Linda Septien working with eleven-year-old singer Kacie Lynch on a song called "Mirror, Mirror." On the page it reads as a monologue, but like any coaching it was actually a conversation: Kacie's part was sung, Septien's was spoken.

Kacie: (sings)

Linda: Okay, it's a dance song, it's not pretty, it's not a power ballad. It moves quick, so be quick. Sing it like a trumpet.

K: (sings)

L: Add a scat on each of the ends—sing it like this: "You know how much he caa-aaares."

K: (sings)

L: Fade the ending—it should be like a balloon running out of air.

K: (sings)

L: Use your diaphragm, not your face. Hold your tongue tighter there for a clearer sound.

K: (sings)

L: Get your cheeks back on the scats . . . almost . . . almost . . . *there* it is.

K: (sings)

L: Use your yawn muscles—you're using wimpy muscles there. *There* it is.

K: (finishes song)

L: That was okay, but I think you've got a better one in you.

K (nodding): Uh-huh.

L: Now you gotta go practice that a bunch bunch bunch bunch bunch.

K: Okay.

This is Septien's GPS reflex in action, producing a linked series of vivid, just-in-time directives that zap the student's skill circuit, guiding it in the right direction. In the space of a three-minute song, Septien sent signals on:

1. The goal/feeling of the whole song ("it's a dance song . . . like a trumpet").
2. The goal/feeling of certain sections (". . . like a balloon; caa-aaares").
3. Highly specific physical moves required to hit certain notes ("cheeks back, tongue tighter, yawn muscles").

4. Motivation/goals ("you've got a better one in you . . . gotta go practice a bunch").

Septien was concise, locating mistakes and their solutions in the same vivid stroke. She highlighted the crucial moments when Kacie hit the desired mark. ("*There* it is.") Septien's skill is not only her matrix of knowledge but also the lightning-fast connections she makes between that matrix and Kacie's efforts, linking where Kacie is now with actions that will take her where she ought to go.*

Patience is a word we use a lot to describe great teachers at work. But what I saw was not patience, exactly. It was more like probing, strategic impatience. The master coaches I met were constantly changing their input. If A didn't work, they tried B and C; if they failed, the rest of the alphabet was holstered and ready. What seemed like patient repetition from the outside was actually, on closer examination, a series of subtle variations, each one a distinct firing, each one creating a worthwhile combination of errors and fixes that grew myelin.

Of the many phrases I heard echoing around the talent hotbeds, one stood out as common to all of them. It was: "Good. Okay, now do_____." A coach would employ it when a student got the hang of some new move or technique. As soon as the student could accomplish the feat (play that chord, hit that volley), the coach would quickly layer in an added difficulty. *Good. Okay, now do it faster. Now do it with the harmony*. Small successes were not stopping points but stepping-stones.

"One of the big things I've learned over the years is to

---

* It must have worked: a few months after this rehearsal, Kacie signed a recording contract with Universal Records.

push," Septien said. "The second they get to a new spot, even if they're still groping a little bit, I push them to the next level."

"Push the buttons, push the buttons, push the buttons, and see what you can do," Lansdorp said. "A mind is such a hands-on kind of thing. It's fantastic!"

THEATRICAL HONESTY: THE FOURTH VIRTUE
Many of the coaches I met radiated a subtle theatrical air. Robert Lansdorp wore a snow-white pompadour and a black leather jacket and spoke in a booming Sinatra baritone. Septien's sheeny outfits and flawless hair evoked a Hollywood star. Larisa Preobrazhenskaya (who trained in her youth as an actress) favored Gloria Swanson turban-style head wraps and spotless white track suits, and could go from a Brezhnev glower to a Betty White smile in a heartbeat. Lansdorp took positive glee in the characterizations he would play. "I'm a to-tal put-on," he said. "I raise my voice, lower my voice, ask questions, figure out how they react. I have all kinds of things I do; sometimes I'm mean and tough, sometimes I'm easygoing. It depends what works for that kid."

It would be easy to conclude, from this pattern, that master coaches traffic in hokum. But the longer I saw them work, the more I saw that drama and character are the tools master coaches use to reach the student with the truth about their performance. As Ron Gallimore said, moral honesty is at the core of the job description—character in the deeper sense of the word. "Truly great teachers connect with students because of who they are as moral standards," he said. "There's an empathy, a selflessness, because you're not trying to tell the student something they know, but are finding, in their effort, a place to make a real connection."

Theatrical honesty works best when teachers are performing their most essential myelinating role: pointing out errors. For example, consider a KIPP math class taught by Lolita Jackson, whom we met earlier. For an hour and forty-five minutes, Jackson worked the room like a master heavy-equipment operator, flicking levers, controlling every move with the instrument of her voice, her body, her eyes. She was warm and encouraging one second, surprised the next, terrifying the next. At one point she found that a student named Geraldo had been figuring the circumference of a circle using the wrong formula.

"So why did you multiply by *four*?" she said, disbelief rising in her voice. Her finger jabbed the paper, a witness identifying a criminal in a lineup. "You had two right there. Right here! That's where you made your error—*right there*. Right there!"

She turned to the class, and her face suddenly became friendly and open. The crime witness was gone, replaced by your kindest aunt. "Who else was confused about that? Don't be shy. I'll make sure you're not confused by the time you leave here."

Midway through class she mentioned that another student, José, who'd been struggling, recently scored well on a test. She walked over and stood close.

"You tell your parents [about the test]?"

José nodded.

"Did they like it? Did they like it? You gonna be like this until the end of the year?"

José said, "Yes, Ms. Jackson."

She looked at him sternly. "You know what, José, I *don't* like it. I don't like it," she said.

The class held its breath, and Ms. Jackson held the moment. Then she released a sunburst of a smile. "I don't like it—I love it! I love it! I LOVE it!"

The class then did the circumference problem again, and again, and once again. First 80 percent of the class got it right, then 90, then 95 percent, then 100 percent, which they celebrated with a group stomp-clap.

"Do we have a better understanding? A better understanding?" Ms. Jackson said, summing up. "You don't have a complete understanding of this, no way, we haven't done it enough. But do we have a better understanding? YES!"

"I can connect with them because I know what I'm talking about," Jackson told me afterward. "I didn't go to college until my kids were in high school, and so I've been on both sides of that. I know the world they live in. This isn't about *math*. I'm not teaching math. It's about *life*. It's about every single day being a new day, and each time you wake up, you look at the sky you've got as a gift. The day is here. What are you going to do with it?"

CIRCUIT-GROWING: WHY TEACHING SOCCER IS DIFFERENT FROM TEACHING VIOLIN

Given the coaches we've met so far, it's tempting to conceptualize a master coach as a busy electrician, always zapping the student with helpful signals, soldering the myelin connections. That is often the case. But many other times the most masterful coaches are completely silent. Consider this conundrum: both Brazilian soccer academies and Suzuki violin instruction programs are remarkably good at developing world-class talent. Yet Brazilian soccer coaches talk very little, while Suzuki violin teachers talk a lot. To see why, let's first look at them one by one.

Brazilian futsal practices are the essence of simplicity. The coach begins with a few cursory drills, then divides the team into two sides and lets them play an intense, full-throttle game, during which the coach rarely says a word. The coach is attentive. He occasionally smiles or laughs or says *oooooooo* for a close play as a fan would. But he doesn't coach in the regular sense of the term, which is to say he doesn't stop the game, teach, praise, critique, or otherwise exert any control whatsoever. On the surface, this laid-back approach would seem to violate the basic precepts of master coaching. How can you build skill if you don't stop the action, give information, praise, and correct?

At the other end of the spectrum is a Suzuki violin lesson. Here the teacher monitors beginners with microscopic precision. Some programs do not permit the student to play a note until she has spent several weeks learning how to hold the bow and violin. (In Japan many Suzuki students aren't allowed even to touch the violin for the first few weeks but are given shoeboxes with strings to practice the holds.) Suzuki training is the photographic negative of Brazilian futsal: it's 100 percent structure and zero free play. Yet judging by impressive results, both coaching techniques (or seeming lack thereof) seem to work extremely well. Why?

The answer lies in at the nature of the skill circuits that each technique is trying to develop. From the myelin point of view, the two coaches only look as if they are doing the opposite thing. In fact, they are both doing precisely what good coaches should do: they are helping the right circuit to fire as often as possible. The difference is the shape of the circuits each is trying to grow.

In skill circuits, as in any electrical circuit, form follows function. Different skills require different patterns of action, thus differently structured circuits. For instance, visualize what's happening inside the nervous system of a soccer player as she moves downfield on a breakaway. The ideal soccer circuitry is varied and fast, changing fluidly in response to each obstacle, capable of producing a myriad of possible options that can fire in liquid succession: now *this, this, this,* and *that.* Speed and flexibility are everything; the faster and more flexible the circuit, the more obstacles can be overcome, and the greater that player's skill. If ideal soccer circuitry were rendered as an electrician's blueprint, it would look like a gargantuan hedge of ivy vines: a vast, interconnected network of equally accessible possibilities (a.k.a. fakes and moves) leading to the same end: Pelé dribbling downfield alone.

Now visualize the circuitry that fires when a violinist plays a Mozart sonata. This circuit is not a vinelike tangle of improvisation but rather a tightly defined series of pathways designed to create—or more accurately, re-create—a single set of ideal movements. Consistency rules; when the violinist plays an A-minor chord, it must always be an A-minor chord, and not a smidgen off. This circuit of precision and stability serves as the foundation on which other, increasingly complex patterns can be constructed to form that Mozart sonata. If ideal violin-playing circuitry were also rendered as an electrician's blueprint, it would look like an oak tree: a solid trunk of technique growing straight upward, branching off into realms of pure fluency—Itzhak Perlman flying through high canopies of sixteenth notes.

During that "uncoached" futsal practice in São Paolo, the players' flexible-skill circuits are firing with great speed and intensity. The game serves as a factory of precisely the sort of encounters that coaches want to teach, along with the benefit of instant feedback: when a move doesn't work, the ball is taken away, and *humiliado* results; when it does work, the result is the ecstasy of a goal. To stop the game in order to highlight some technical detail or give praise would be to interrupt the flow of attentive firing, failing, and learning that is the heart of flexible-circuit deep practice. The lessons the players teach themselves are more powerful than anything the coach might say.*

The beginner violinist represents the opposite case. Here the circuit needs not just to be fired but to be fired correctly. The high level of coaching input is a reflection of a crucial physiological fact: this circuit will form the core of the oak's trunk. The coach's actions form a kind of trellis, to direct the seedling's growth precisely where it needs to go. (Which doesn't mean the process needs to be unnecessarily solemn, by the way. The Suzuki teachers I've met are charming and charismatic, able to turn holding a shoebox into an enjoyable game.)

Skills like soccer, writing, and comedy are flexible-circuit skills, meaning that they require us to grow vast ivy-vine circuits that we can flick through to navigate an ever-changing set of obstacles. Playing violin, golf, gymnastics, and figure skating, on the other hand, are consistent-circuit skills, depending utterly on a solid foundation of technique that enables us to reliably re-create the fundamentals of an ideal performance. (This is why self-taught violinists, skaters, and gymnasts rarely reach world-class level and why self-taught

---

* It's also a lot more fun—a point not lost on Fernando, the twenty-something son of Emilio Miranda, the professor of soccer at the University of São Paolo. Fernando went to college in Virginia and came back mystified by the coach's role in the game. "In America, everyone is yelling all the time. Telling the kids, 'Shoot the ball, pass the ball!' I once saw a kid wearing a shirt that said 'THERE ARE NO EASY DAYS.'" Fernando made a confused face. "No easy days, when you're ten? The play should be easy, fun, nice. To be so serious is not good."

novelists, comedians, and soccer players do all the time.) The universal rule remains the same: good coaching supports the desired circuit. The passive Brazilian coach and the highly in-volved Suzuki teacher only seem to use different methods; when we look closer, we see that their goal is the same as that of John Wooden or Mary Epperson or any other master coach: to get inside the deep-practice zone, to maximize the firings that grow the right myelin for the task, and ultimately to move closer toward the day that every coach desires, when the students become their own teachers.

"If it's a choice between me telling them to do it, or them figuring it out, I'll take the second option every time," Lansdorp said. "You've got to make the kid an independent thinker, a problem-solver. I don't need to see them every day, for chrissake. You can't keep breast-feeding them all the time. The point is, they've got to figure things out for themselves."

Chapter 10

Tom Martinez and the $60 Million Bet

A teacher is one who makes himself
progressively unnecessary.
—Thomas Carruthers

Master coaches, like NASA engineers, are familiar with irony. They spend years painstakingly helping to construct talent, then are left behind, gazing upward when the rocket lifts off. For every celebrated coaching star like John Wooden, there are dozens of Hans Jensens, Mary Eppersons, and Larisa Preobrazhenskayas who help grow world-class talent and yet live in obscurity.*

There are exceptions to this rule, however, unexpected moments when the world's spotlight shines on the subtle art of the master coach. One of these moments happened not so long ago in northern California. The coach was Tom Martinez, and the reason was that the Oakland Raiders football team was facing a $60 million problem.

---

* Not that they are unhappy with this role. Of the coaches I met, only the outspoken Lansdorp ever expressed anything like disgruntlement, and even that was comic. ("If Maria [Sharapova] doesn't buy me a new car," he said, "I'm going to shoot myself.")

Thanks to their bumbling 2–14 won-lost record the previous year, the Raiders had won the National Football League's first prize for ineptitude: the right to choose the most talented college player in the nation. Unfortunately, Raiders management wasn't sure who that player might be. They'd narrowed the possibilities to two. Option A was Calvin Johnson, a wide receiver from Georgia Tech University. Johnson stood six foot five, weighed 239 pounds, and possessed an unearthly combination of speed and body control that inspired awed scouts to christen him the Michael Jordan of football. "In everybody's mind, Calvin Johnson is the safest pick in this draft," said Mike Mayock, an NFL Network analyst.

Option B was a six-foot-five-inch, 259-pound question mark named JaMarcus Russell. A few months earlier Russell had been a mere blip on scouting radar screens. He had begun his junior season as a backup quarterback at Louisiana State University and had surprised most observers by declaring for the draft after an impressive year. The film and scouting reports, thin as they were, looked tantalizing. On the one hand, Russell possessed a freakishly strong arm (he could throw 60 yards from his knees) along with a painterly touch on short passes and a knack for performing under pressure. On the other hand, the NFL cellar was littered with franchises wrecked by phantom quarterback talent. Inside Raiders headquarters in Alameda, passionate arguments were waged: half the team's executives wanted Johnson, half wanted Russell.

This was a $60 million bet, with the future of the franchise at stake. So the Raiders' front office did the only thing they could do. They analyzed all the data—intelligence tests, scouting reports, film, stats. Then they chucked all the data in the trash can and phoned Tom Martinez.

Officially Tom Martinez is a retired junior college coach.

For thirty-two years he'd headed the women's basketball and softball and men's football programs at San Mateo College, winning fourteen hundred games in all without a single losing season. Unofficially, Martinez is a quarterback guru. His best-known student is a kid he calls Tommy, better known to the world as Tom Brady, a three-time Super Bowl–winning quarterback for the New England Patriots. Martinez started working with Brady when Brady was a gawky thirteen-year-old. Their relationship can be measured by the list of Martinez technique tips that Brady carries on a slip in his wallet, and by the fact that Brady has returned to Martinez three or four times a year for the past seventeen years for tune-ups.

Martinez may have been retired, but demand for his services was on the upswing. In fact, a few months before the draft, Martinez had been quietly approached by JaMarcus Russell's agent, who asked him if he could work with Russell, prepping the LSU star for his pre-draft workouts.

This situation was unique, to say the least. Parties on both sides of the most high-stakes sports decision of the year had sought out the wisdom of the same anonymous ex-junior-college coach who would otherwise be spending his days puttering about the garden.

"Life's funny, isn't it?" Martinez said. He laughed when asked about the Raiders call. "They knew nothing about Russell. Nobody did. He was a blank slate." Martinez was entertained, and as with every emotion, he communicated his entertainment clearly. His leonine head tipped and shook; his eyes shone with happy disbelief. "He's what they can't figure out: a big, quiet black kid. So they call some guy in a San Mateo College sweatshirt."

We're sitting in his kitchen on a faultlessly beautiful Saturday in May. Martinez has suffered ill health—diabetes and blood pressure problems—but appears tan and strong, if slow on his feet. He's six foot one and handsome in the way of a 1940s movie star: he has large, expressive eyes under dark eyebrows, an imperial Roman nose, a strong chin. It's a mountain range of a face, one that moods travel across like weather. I ask him how he went about coaching a player like Russell, whom he'd never met before the call from Russell's agent.

"With a new kid, it's no different from meeting a girl you might want to go on a date with," Martinez said. "You make eye contact, and there's something happening there, underneath. Something hits a nerve, something is transmitted through eye contact that tells you to say hello. That's what I look for first in a kid, something to take our connection to a potentially different spot."

Martinez pauses, checking to make sure I'm understanding.

"When I got to Arizona, I met JaMarcus. Right off he's suspicious, of course. He's got to be. Everybody's trying to get something from him. I tell him who I am, and he starts off with a lot of 'yes sir, yes sir, no sir.' Real polite. But formal. Distant. And that's not gonna work."

Martinez leans in. His gaze goes gunfighter-level.

"I told him, 'Look, JaMarcus, I appreciate you more than you can understand. But I'm not going to kiss your ass. You can listen to what I have to say or not. If I'm full of shit, then you can decide I'm full of shit. I'm an old man. I don't need you to make my reputation. But there's just one thing I want from you.'

"When JaMarcus heard that, his eyes got real narrow. He tightened up. He was thinking, 'Uh-oh, here it comes.' And I told him, 'I want a signed jersey and photo for my grandson.' And that's when JaMarcus smiled." Martinez smiled hugely.

"JaMarcus says, 'That's it?' I look at him and I say, 'That's it. That's what I want.' We got along pretty good after that."

Let's take a moment and consider what Martinez was describing here. The question was about coaching, and yet he did not describe anything related to football, or anything even remotely physical. Instead he described, with a novelist's sensitivity to timing and mood, a delicate human connection of language, gesture, and emotion. Martinez did not plan or script this connection—he figured it out on the fly. When he met Russell, he was able to reach into his matrix of knowledge and to improvise, in the space of thirty seconds, a bridge of trust and respect. No wonder he picked the analogy of romance—or, as he later put it in safecracker terms that would have pleased Baron Lamm, "I need to get access to their learning process."

Connection is important, but it's not the only thing. To show me how he worked with Russell, Martinez invited me to one of his weekend coaching clinics. We drove a few minutes to a nearby high school field where six quarterbacks waited. The youngest was thirteen, the oldest seventeen. They shifted their bodies uneasily, their limbs still too long for their frames, their eyes darty. They looked like deer. Martinez went right to work.

First, Martinez had them review a three-step dropback, as they did every Saturday. He lined them up and, like a dance instructor, called out the rhythm: pop, reach, step, roll, push. He counted, and they did it, and Martinez fired his corrections at individual players.

"Get the ball back faster. The ball's on fire, and you got to get it out."

"Keep the ball high; it's like an airplane taking off."

"The ball goes from butt to armpit."

"Get your feet apart—be an athlete, now."

"You're like a waiter. Keep the ball up, deliver it."

"Your left foot is killing you, know what I mean? You're understepping. You got to roll and pop."

"See how easy it isn't?"

In thirty seconds he explained the correct dropback motion in four distinct ways: tactile ("ball on fire"), personification ("waiter"), image ("airplane"), and physical ("butt to armpit"). He moved on to other drills. Each was elemental in its simplicity, taking a chunk of the quarterbacking circuit and isolating it, to better reveal and correct mistakes. The group threw square-outs and buttonhooks, and finished with a drill that was straight out of Tom Brady's wallet: throwing down the hall. One person stood between quarterback and receiver with his arms up; the goal was to throw down the alleyway formed by the arms. It was dead-simple, and Martinez coached on every repetition.

"Finish. Alex, you're all arm. Finish the throw."

"You just threw an interception, son. Now the other team's band is playing."

"You're all arm-strong, strong enough to do it wrong. Now control the point, use the body."

"Take pride in your throw, for goodness' sake."

Afterward we drove to a nearby restaurant and got hamburgers. A baseball game was on television. The crowd was college students, half of them on cell phones and iPods. Martinez's eyes took them in.

"Kids today are hard to reach," he said. "They know how to give all the right answers, all the programmed answers. So when I see things, I say it so you can hear it. I say it a lot. Each guy has his own button you can tap on. Who are you out here for? If it's what *you* want, fine, we can do that. If you're out here because of your father or you think it's cool, it's going to take a lot longer. These things are not flu shots. It takes work. It's like the violin. There's no magic to it. If you don't practice, you'll never play the tune.

"Sixty percent of what you teach applies to everybody," he continued. "The trick is how you get that sixty percent to the person. If I teach you, I'm concerned about what you think and how you think. I want to teach you how to learn in a way that's right for you. My greatest challenge is not teaching Tom Brady but some guy who can't do it at all, and getting them to a point where they can. Now *that* is coaching."

Martinez took a bite of his hamburger. "With JaMarcus, I worked with him for maybe twenty days. I was basically putting some polish on a great car. We did all the stuff you saw out there today. Throwing drills. Dropbacks. Patterns. Down-the-hall drills. If it got too dry, I'd say something funny, mix it up a little. We just did a simple, regular, straightforward tune-up. Then we scripted a workout he'd do for the scouts. I also spent time with him, his family. I tried to answer the questions: Does he listen? Is he smart? What's his work ethic? What's his commitment? It's all there. He has good solid values. I met his uncle Ray, who's a tremendous guy, a role model, a good man. When the Raiders asked me, I told them my opinion: this guy could be the Shaquille O'Neal of football."

On March 14, 2007, more than a hundred NFL personnel, including three head coaches and four general managers, converged on Baton Rouge, Louisiana, to watch Russell's official pre-draft workout. Over the next hour or so Russell threw sixty-five balls and every possible pass and missed only five. "He did all the rollouts and dropbacks. We hid nothing,"

Martinez said. "We wanted to show that his perceived weaknesses weren't weaknesses." When it was over, San Diego Chargers general manager A. J. Smith called Russell "the most impressive quarterback I've ever seen in my life." Six weeks later the Raiders selected Russell with the number-one pick in the draft. When the press asked why, head coach Lane Kiffin recited virtually word for word the assessment Martinez had given them, a tribute that entertained Martinez. "Why the hell do the Raiders listen to me? I'm not a brand name," he said. "I'm just some Joe."

But the Raiders listened to Martinez because he possesses a valuable and rare talent. He can walk up to someone he's never met, in an atmosphere thick with unknowns and money and wariness, and forge a connection. He can use that connection to find the truth about someone whose talent is yet to be known to the world and maybe even to himself.

As the sun set, Martinez and I sat in his driveway. We talked about his college teams, his work with Brady, his family. He gave me advice about coaching baseball. ("Teach cutoffs and bunt coverage in a small space. Don't even use a ball—the mental part is all that counts.") He sketched diagrams, checking me at each point to make sure I understood. "I flat-out love coaching," he said toward the end. "There's something there that's real. You get your hands on it, and you can make somebody better than they were. That's one hell of a feeling."

At the meeting with the Raiders, Martinez said, he gave the coaches a piece of advice about how to handle Russell. "For the first three years he'll need a coach who's consistent in vocabulary and method. After three years he'll probably have the experience and knowledge to play. But you can't just give a guy sixty million bucks and say, hey, go win games, go get in the Hall of Fame. He needs mentoring. He needs consistency. He needs *somebody*." The old coach's voice thickened with emotion. He looked into the trees for a moment, cleared his throat. "JaMarcus is like anybody else: he can't do it by himself."

Epilogue: The Myelin World

If we were to diagram the talent code, it would look like this.

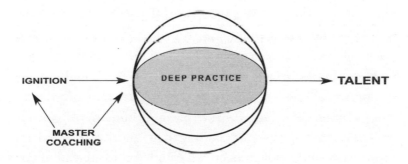

The useful thing about this model is that it's as flexible as myelin itself, applying to all skills, in contexts as small as families and as large as nations. I'd like to end by briefly showing how the code applies to other areas of life, specifically to the ways in which we educate our kids, work, grow older, parent—and even master social skills. We began this book with the promise to use the talent code as a pair of X-ray glasses. Now we'll see how well it works as a telescope.

EDUCATION

For the last forty years or so American education has been divided by what's become known as the Reading Wars. On one side stand the traditionalist forces of Phonics, who believe that the best way to learn to read is through memorizing the sounds of letters and letter-groups. On the other side are the followers of Whole Language, a theory founded in the 1970s that says all children possess the innate ability to read and write, which arrives according to fixed developmental stages. They believe the teacher's role is to be, as the saying goes, "a guide on the side, not a sage on the stage."

For much of the 1980s Whole Language was on the ascent. "Matching letters with sounds is a flat-earth view of the world," wrote Kenneth Goodman in *What's Whole in Whole Language*. Schools started providing literacy-rich environments of books, words, and stories where kids could express this presumably innate ability. Meaning was emphasized over mere sound; systematic instruction in grammar was considered passé. Students were encouraged to ignore errors and use invented spelling. The movement caught on in education circles, and politicians trotted after. In 1987 California mandated Whole Language for teaching reading and writing.

For middle- and upper-income kids, Whole Language seemed to help, or at least not to obviously hurt. For minority and low-income kids, however, it was an unqualified disaster.

By the early 1990s California's scores on the National
Assessment of Educational Progress ranked lower than every
state's but Louisiana. Other states that adopted Whole Language
experienced similar test-score drops. In 1998 two major research efforts, the National Research Council and the National
Reading Panel, found that the lack of Phonics contributed to
lower rates of achievement for most students. Charles Sykes
writes in *Dumbing Down Our Kids* of a fourth grader who received above-average grades and a teacher's comment of
"Wow!" for writing, "I'm going to has majik skates. Im goin
to go to disenelan. Im goin to bin my mom and dad and brusr
and sisd. We r go to se mickey mouse."

Accordingly, the pendulum whipped back toward Phonics.
Defenders of Whole Language have retrenched, incorporat-
ing Phonics into their theories but still lobbying for the essential truth of their view. Phonics supporters, on the other hand,
point to their own list of promising programs. All of which
leaves many teachers and schools wading through piles of
seemingly contradictory theories and wondering who's right.

Looking at the question through the prism of the talent
code, the answer is clear. The relationship between Phonics
and Whole Language precisely mirrors the relationship between deep practice and ignition. Phonics is about building
reliable circuits, paying attention to errors, and fixing them.
It's about chunking: breaking down a skill into its component
parts, and practicing and repeating each action involved in
that skill. It's about the systematic firing of the signals that
build the trusty high-speed skill circuits you're using right
now.

Whole Language, on the other hand, is about ignition,
about filling motivational fuel tanks by creating environments

where children fall in love with reading and writing. Like any ignition, Whole Language can create acceleration for those who already have the inclination and opportunity to deep-practice, but it is worthless to those who don't. To understand myelin is to understand that the Reading Wars should not be a war. Students need both to succeed.

Another education question worth asking is, why are Finnish kids so smart? Finnish teens outscore the rest of the world on the Program for International Student Assessment, despite the fact that Finland's student culture (in contrast to some other high-achieving countries) resembles that of the United States in many ways. As the *Wall Street Journal* noted, Finnish students "waste hours online. They dye their hair, love sarcasm, and listen to rap and heavy metal. But by ninth grade they're way ahead in math, science, and reading—and on track to keeping Finns among the world's most productive workers." What's more, Finns spend less per student than do Americans, $7,500 per year compared with $8,700. While some observers explain the success by pointing to Finland's tradition of self-discipline and the homogeneity of its population, that explanation doesn't wash. Until the 1980s, with those advantages present, Finnish education was generally regarded as average. So what changed?

"Three reasons," Kaisu Karkkainen, principal of the Arabia Comprehensive School in Helsinki, told the *Washington Post*. "Teachers, teachers, and teachers."

In Finland, a teacher is regarded as the social equal of a doctor or lawyer, and is compensated accordingly. All elementary teachers have master's degrees in pedagogy; schools are run like teaching hospitals, where young teachers are analyzed and evaluated. It's competitive: some schools receive forty applications for a single job opening. Thanks to a receptive culture and an intelligent mix of planning and investment, Finland seems to have found a way to institutionalize the deep practice of teaching.

"The key isn't how much money is invested; it's the people," said Finnish author and philosopher Pekka Himanen. "The high quality of Finnish education depends on the high quality of Finnish teachers. . . . Many of the best students want to be teachers. This is linked to the fact that we really believe we live in an information age, so it is respected to be in such a key information profession as teaching."

Finally, here's a third educational question to view through the myelin lens: do baby-brain DVDs such as Baby Einstein (the forerunner of the now-$500 million industry) make children smarter? The conventional-wisdom view of talent would naturally lead one to answer yes. After all, if talent is inborn, then watching these DVDs, with their simple, mesmeric sequences of colorful shapes and light, would presumably help develop a baby's brain (not to mention help a busy parent find a moment of peace).

But studies show that baby-brain DVDs don't make children smarter. In fact, they make them less smart. A 2007 University of Washington study found that, for children aged eight to sixteen months, each hour spent per day viewing "brain science" baby DVDs decreased vocabulary acquisition by 17 percent. And when you think about it in terms of the myelin model, this makes perfect sense. Baby-brain DVDs don't work because they don't create deep practice—in fact, they actively prevent it, by taking up time that could be used for firing circuits. The images and sounds on the DVDs wash over the babies like a warm bath—entertaining and immersive but useless compared with the rich interactions, errors, and learning that happens when babies are staggering around in the real world. Or, to put it another way: *Skill is insulation that wraps neural circuits and grows according to certain signals.*

BUSINESS

When it comes to the production of high-concept metaphors, few areas in life can compete with the business-advice industry. Good organizations, its gurus tell us, are like sports teams playing a game. Or they're like ships sailing a dangerous ocean. Or a team of Everest climbers, or warring Greek cities, or any number of other intricately structured, enticingly dramatic analogies, all of which come with their own sets of roles, rules, and frameworks for improvement, and all of which are more or less true, depending.

Myelin gives us a different model, one that chucks the metaphorical decoration and simply says that good organizations are made of myelin, period. Businesses are groups of people who are building and honing skill circuits in exactly the same way as the tennis players at Spartak or the violinists at Meadowmount. The more an organization embraces the core principles of ignition, deep practice, and master coaching, the more myelin it will build, the more success it will have.

Thirty years ago Toyota was a middling-size car company. Now it is the world's largest automaker. Most analysts attribute Toyota's success to its strategy of *kaizen*, which is Japanese for "continuous improvement" and which just as easily could be called corporate deep practice. *Kaizen* is the process of finding and improving small problems. Each employee, from the janitor on up, has authority to halt the production line if they spot a problem. (Each factory has pull cords on the factory floor, called *andons*.) The vast majority of improvements come from employees, and the vast majority of those changes are small: a one-foot shift in the location of a parts bin, for instance. But they add up. It's estimated that each year Toyota implements around a thousand tiny fixes in each of its assembly lines, about a million tiny fixes over-all. Toyota, moving in these fitful baby steps, is like a giant, car-making Clarissa. The small changes are like tiny wraps of myelin, helping its circuitry run a fraction faster, smoother, and more accurately. The sign over the door of Toyota's Georgetown, Kentucky, factory puts it in perfect deep-practice language: "When something goes wrong, ask WHY five times."

This sounds like a simple thing to do. But in fact, like all deep practice, one first has to overcome the natural tendency to smooth over problems—something particularly difficult in business. James Wiseman, who's now Toyota's vice president for corporate affairs, told *Fast Company* magazine about his first days at the company. At his previous jobs, he said, "there was always a lot of looking for the silver bullet, looking for the big, dramatic improvement." When he arrived at Toyota, he realized things were different. "One Friday I gave a report of an activity we'd been doing [a plant expansion], and I spoke very positively about it, I bragged a little. After two or three minutes, I sat down. And Mr. Cho [Fujio Cho, now the chairman of Toyota worldwide] kind of looked at me. I could see he was puzzled. He said, 'Jim-san. We all know you are a good manager, otherwise we would not have hired you. But please talk to us about your problems so we can all work on them together.'"

PSYCHOLOGY

The Shyness Clinic is located in a nondescript office park on a busy road in Palo Alto, California. It has slate-gray walls and dull burgundy furniture; the only sign of life is an underwater photograph of a clownfish peeping warily from the safety of an anemone's tentacles. The clinic is built around the idea that social skills are just like any other skill. Founders Philip Zimbardo and Lynne Henderson call their concept social-fitness training—we might call it myelination through deep practice.

"We believe that people are shy not because they lack social skills but because they haven't practiced them sufficiently," said therapist Nicole Shiloff. "Talking on the phone or asking someone on a date is a learnable skill, exactly like a tennis forehand. The key is that people have to linger in that uncomfortable area, learn to tolerate the anxiety. If you practice, you can get to the level you want." The godfather of this kind of therapy is Dr. Albert Ellis. Ellis, who was born in 1913 and raised in the Bronx, was a painfully shy teenager, unable to bring himself to speak to women. But one afternoon he decided to make a change. He sat on a bench near the New York Botanical Garden and chatted with every woman who sat down. In one month he spoke with 130 women. "Thirty walked away immediately," he said. "I talked with the other hundred, for the first time in my life, no matter how anxious I was. Nobody vomited and ran away. Nobody called the cops."

Ellis, who went on to write dozens of books, built a straight-talk, action-oriented approach that challenged the Freudian model of examining childhood experience. "Neurosis is just a high-class word for whining," he said. "The trouble with most therapy is that it helps you to feel better. But you don't get better. You have to back it up with action, action, action."

Ellis's approach, combined with that of Dr. Aaron Beck, became known as cognitive-behavioral therapy, which has been shown, according to *The New York Times*, to be equal to or better than prescription drugs for combating depression, anxiety, and obsessive-compulsive disorder. As Ellis liked to point out, his ideas weren't new: they came from the Stoic philosophers like Epictetus, who said, "It's not events, but our opinions about them, which cause us suffering." Ellis, who died in 2007, was named the second most influential psychologist of the twentieth century by the American Psychological Association. (Carl Rogers was first, Freud was third.)

The Shyness Clinic session I attended, which included eight clinically shy people, was typical. There was no talk about anybody's past, no attempt to deconstruct the root causes of shyness. There was only practice and feedback, overseen by Shiloff's gentle but tough-minded coaching, correcting any inaccurate perceptions and pushing them to try harder, once more. It was like being at Meadowmount, Spartak, or any other talent hotbed.

The clients start by attempting to master easier challenges: role-playing water-cooler chat and phone calls. Over several months, they gradually progress to harder tasks, such as asking for a date. At the program's highest level, they perform Olympian feats of outgoingness such as purposely embarrassing themselves by dropping a watermelon in the middle of a crowded supermarket. The point, Shiloff explained, is to fire the circuit and thus to linger in the discomfort a little longer each time. It is the staggering-baby process all over again, although the clinic has more suitable ways to describe the sensation. One of Shiloff's clients, a college student I'll call David, compared his progress to moving up on levels of a video game. "At first it seems really confusing, like everything's coming at you from all angles," he said. "But then you sort of figure it out, and pretty soon it feels natural."

A smiling twenty-six-year-old computer tech named Andre told me he hadn't talked to a woman for months before enrolling at the Shyness Clinic. Now he had just gone on three dates and signed up for a ballroom-dancing class. "When I thought I was born this way, then I thought, what's the use," Andre said. "But when it's a skill, everything changes."

Deep practice and myelin are also behind the success of Virtual Iraq, a new technique being used to help U.S. soldiers who suffer post-traumatic stress disorder, a condition where an everyday event (the sound of a car backfiring, or footsteps) triggers painfully debilitating memories. Virtual Iraq uses videogamelike software to help patients experience a vivid re-creation of their trauma, complete with smells, sounds, and sensations. The idea is to relive the memory and rob it of its power, a technique therapists call prolonged exposure therapy.

Virtual Iraq operates exactly like the Shyness Clinic, or any other talent hotbed for that matter. The desired skill is to experience traumatic events (footsteps, loud noises) without triggering the debilitating connection. They can't unbuild the circuit (remember, myelin only wraps; it doesn't unwrap), so the best way to gain the new skill is to establish and deep-practice a new circuit that connects the traumatic stimulus to normal, everyday events. It's difficult at first. But the more the clients fire that circuit, the better they get at firing it. As one treated soldier told *The New Yorker*, "Most of the intrusive thoughts have gone away. You never really get rid of PTSD, but you learn to live with it. I had pictures of my [dead] team leader that I couldn't look at for three years. They're up on my wall now."

AGING

The stack of research on cognition and aging keeps growing, each new study chiming in with the same refrain: *use it or lose it*. The clinical phrase is "cognitive reserve," which sounds abstract until George Bartzokis wraps a cloth napkin tightly around a pen to explain what's really going on. The pen is the nerve fiber, and the napkin is the myelin. The aging of the brain, Bartzokis explains, is when gaps start appearing in the napkin.

"The myelin literally starts to split apart with age," Bartzokis said. "This is why every old person you've ever met in your life moves more slowly than they did when they were younger. Their muscles haven't changed, but the speed of the impulses they can send to them has changed, because the myelin gets old."

The good news is that while natural waves of myelination end in our thirties, our overall volume of myelin increases until our fifties, and we always retain the ability to add more myelin through deep practice. "You must remember the myelin is alive, always being generated and degenerating, like a war," Bartzokis says. "When we are younger, we build myelin easily. As we age the overall balance shifts toward degeneration, but we can keep adding myelin. Even when the myelin is breaking up, we can still build it, right to the end of our lives."

This is why level of education is one of the most reliable predictors for Alzheimer's onset, Bartzokis says. More education creates a thicker, more robust circuit, better able to compensate for the early phases of disease. It's also why we've recently seen an avalanche of new studies, books, and video games built on the myelin-centric principle that practice staves off cognitive decline. The myelin model also highlights the importance of seeking new challenges. Experiments have found that situations in which people are forced to adapt and attune themselves to new challenges (i.e., make errors, pay attention, deep-practice) tend to increase cognitive reserve. One study showed that elderly people who pursued more leisure activities had a 38 percent lower risk for developing dementia. As one neurologist pointed out, the mantra "Use it or lose it" needs an update. It should be "Use it and get more of it."

Bringing It Home

Like a lot of parents, my wife Jen and I spent an undue portion of our kids' early lives keeping an eye out for omens. As our four kids crawled, toddled, and ran, we wondered what secret talents lay in store. *Is he or she destined to be a musician? An athlete? A scientist?* This kind of thinking has its positive aspects—it's exciting to believe that your child arrives prewired with special talents. But it's also based on some false assumptions and certainly sets up false expectations that, among other things, make for a heck of a lot of driving. Art lessons? Why not! Hockey camp? Dance class? Gymnastics? Yes! When you're caretaker for a mysterious gift, you have no justifiable reason to turn down an opportunity that might allow that gift to be expressed.

But when you think about talent as myelin—when you visualize those tiny strings of Christmas lights, when you look for hair-trigger moments of ignition, when you tune into the teaching signals you send—life changes. Like most big changes, this one shows itself in small ways. Like when our son, Aidan, has a tough new song on the piano, and Jen encourages him to try the first five notes over and over, doing it in baby steps until it starts to click. Or when our daughters Katie and Lia are skiing, and they excitedly inform us that they fell a bunch of times, which must be a sign that they are getting better. (The concept works considerably better with skiing than it will with learning to drive a car.) Or maybe it's when our three girls, in a burst of Brontë-like scribblemania, started writing stories and letters for each other, and how Jen leaves out colored pencils and notebooks to fuel their frenzy of composition. Mostly, though, I feel it in a changed attitude toward failure, which doesn't feel like a setback or the writing on the wall anymore, but like a path forward.

Last summer Zoe, our youngest, was all set to start piano lessons. She enjoyed plunking around on the keyboard; her sisters had shown her how to play a couple of songs. Then one afternoon Zoe started talking about violins—how pretty they sounded, and how she wanted one. Where this idea came from, we're not sure. (Was it the bluegrass concert she saw? Her friend who played violin?) But we picked up a used violin and found a good Suzuki teacher. Long story short, our family dinners now feature a pint-size strolling violinist (who is not shy about requesting monetary tips).

Carol Dweck, the psychologist who studies motivation, likes to say that all the world's parenting advice can be distilled to two simple rules: pay attention to what your children are fascinated by, and praise them for their effort. To which I would add, tell them how the myelin mechanism works, as Dweck herself did in a study that revealed the power of sending this message. She began by splitting seven hundred low-achieving middle schoolers into two groups. The first were given an eight-week workshop of study skills; the second were given the identical workshop along with something extra: a special fifty-minute session that described how the brain grows when it's challenged. Within a semester the second group had significantly improved their grades and study habits. The experimenters didn't tell the teachers which group the kids were in, but the teachers could tell anyway. The teachers couldn't put their finger on it, but they knew something big had changed.

Last June I was asked to coach our town's Little League all-star team of eleven- and twelve-year-old boys. The job was not highly coveted, for good reason. In Homer, where we live, the all-star tournament held a long tradition of spectacular failures. For most of the past decade the tournament had followed the same plotline as the Boston Massacre: our small seaboard town (scrappy, scrawny, ill armed) against well-drilled, sleekly uniformed squadrons from larger, far-off communities. Two years earlier we'd lost every game by ten runs or more.

With only thirty kids in the town league and three weeks to practice, my two fellow coaches and I couldn't afford to be choosy. Our roster of twelve thus included a small core of solid players and a generous helping of younger players who were relatively new to the sport. Sam, who played outfield and first base, had a swing that resembled a person fighting off a wolverine. Ghen, who preferred wearing a stocking hat to a baseball cap, wasn't too sure about some of the rules, like whether a base runner should run on a fly ball. Several others were wary of the ball—for good reason, since Ben was sporting two black eyes and a broken nose, a souvenir from an ill-advised game of three-way catch. At the first practice, as the players warmed up by playing catch, the other coaches and I posed a challenge: could every pair make ten good throws and catches without dropping or overthrowing the ball? After fifteen minutes, we decided it would be best to move on to another drill.

There was, as the saying goes, only one thing to do. Like Mike Feinberg and Dave Levin at KIPP, I followed the Butch Cassidy method. For the next three weeks I stole ideas from the people and places I'd been visiting over the past year and, with the other coaches, applied them to our team.

Like the music teachers at Meadowmount, we taught hitting by slowing the swings down, working on a tee, and having the players watch and imitate good swings over and over.

Like John Wooden or Linda Septien, we tried to teach with quick, informative, GPS-style bursts. In my previous years of coaching, I'd always coached the group as a whole, teaching one way for everyone. Now I tried to target each player, finding ways to connect and, when they did something correctly, stopping them and telling them to remember that feeling.

Like the Brazilian futsal players, we found ways to compress and speed up the game. We pitched batting practice from 30 feet away instead of 45, forcing our hitters to react more quickly.

Like Tom Martinez, we taught defensive positioning by laying out a miniature baseball field and isolating the mental element of the game —who covers first on a bunt, who has the cutoff to a play at home. I shamelessly channeled Martinezisms. *Finish the throw. Take pride in your swing. See how easy it isn't?*

When the day came, we rented an RV and drove north to Kenai, host city for the four-day-long tournament. We set up a campsite at the ball field and quickly assembled our secret weapons: the lucky polar bear doll, the salmon pregame meal, and the assortment of rubber bands and braids my daughters used to lend the team its distinctive, Björk-like hairstyles. We felt prepared. But when our first opponent, Kodiak, trotted smoothly onto the field, our team suddenly looked twitchy and nervous. So did their parents in the stands, some of whom had witnessed last year's contest versus Kodiak, in which we'd been thumped 15–1. Kodiak whipped through a well-choreographed warm-up routine. We watched in silence. "They're go-ooood," Ben said in awe.

As if to prove it, Kodiak's leadoff hitter opened the game by laying down a perfect bunt that rolled softly down the third-base line—a sure hit. But it wasn't. Brian, our third baseman, charged, scooped the ball with his bare hand, and whipped it to first, where Johan, the second baseman, was waiting to make the out, just like we'd practiced. We held them scoreless for three innings, then scored two runs on a pair of hard-hit balls to take the lead. Kodiak replied with four runs, and then we came back when Brian, to his astonishment as well as ours, whacked an Andruw Jones–worthy home run over the left-field fence. It was a tight, thrilling, well-played game that ended just short of a win. Nevertheless, the team walked back to the campsite shocked and happy at what we'd done. We felt the strange thrill of the HSE. As one of the parents said, "It's like a miracle."

It would be nice to say that we miraculously won the tournament. We didn't. We played well, winning one and losing two more heart-stoppingly close games, one in extra innings. Each game was studded with revelatory moments: Ghen ripping a single, Aidan pitching shutout ball, Ben making fearless catches, and Sam, the ex-wolverine-fighter, hitting a home run. And when the last game was over and the campsite was taken down, a few members of the team were still on the field playing pickup games in their uniforms. They would have played all night.

When I started working on this project, I came across an electron microscope photo of myelin. It's not a great image in the usual sense of the word: it's grainy and blurred. But I like looking at it, because you can see each individual wrap, like the layers in a cliff face or the growth rings of a tree. Each wrap of myelin is a unique tracing of some past event. Perhaps that wrap was caused by a coach's pointer; perhaps that one by a parent's encouraging glance; perhaps that one by hearing a song they loved. In the whorls of myelin resides a person's secret history, the flow of interactions and influences that make up a life, the Christmas lights that, for some reason, lit up.

At home, I find myself picturing these strings of light sometimes, flickering and flashing as our family plays games, gets lost in books, or talks around the dinner table. It seems utterly impossible that these little people will soon be grown up, doing unthinkably complicated and marvelous things, but it's not. It will happen. After all, we are myelin beings.

The other day our daughter Zoe picked up her violin and stumbled her way through a new song about a fat king and queen who had a dog. She stopped frequently. She made mistakes. She started over. It sounded choppy, and it sounded wonderful. "I'm going to practice it a zillion million times," she said. "I'm going to play super good."

Notes on Sources

Introduction

For more on Clarissa and her high-velocity practice, see Gary E. McPherson and James M. Renwick, "Interest and Choice: Student-Selected Repertoire and Its Effect on Practising Behavior," *British Journal of Music Education* 19 (June 2002), 173–88, and "I've Got to Do My Scales First!" *Proceedings of the Sixth International Conference on Music Perception and Cognition* (Keele, Staffordshire, U.K.: Keele University Department of Psychology, 2000), CD-ROM.

Chapter 1: The Sweet Spot

While our intuition tells us that prodigies are destined for greatness, a mountain of scientific data shows otherwise. For more, see Benjamin Bloom's "The Role of Gifts and Markers in the Development of Talent," *Exceptional Children* 48 (1982), 510–21; and Lauren A. Sosniak's "Developing Talent: Time, Task, and Context" in N. Colangelo and G. Davis's *Handbook of Gifted Education* (New York: Allyn & Bacon, 2003). For good case studies on this topic, see Rena Subotnik, Lee Kassan, Ellen Summers, and Alan Wasser's long-term study of high-IQ students at a New York school for the gifted in *Genius Revisited: High IQ Children Grown Up* (Norwood, N.J.: Ablex, 1993) or the many accounts of Stanford psychologist Lewis Terman's long-term studies of high-IQ children. For an excellent and far-reaching overview of this topic and more, see Malcolm Gladwell's *Outliers: The Story of Success* (New York: Little, Brown, 2008).

Robert Bjork's notion of "the sweet spot" of learning was conceptualized by others, most prominently by Russian psychologist Lev Vygotsky in the 1920s, who gave it a slightly less catchy name: the zone of proximal development. For more on Bjork's work on desirable difficulties, see "Memory and Metamemory Considerations in the Training of Human Beings," in *Metacognition: Knowing About Knowing* (Cambridge, Mass.: MIT Press, 1994), 185–205, and "Assessing Our Own Competence: Heuristics and Illusions," *Attention and Performance XVII. Cognitive Regulation of Performance: Interaction of Theory and Application* (Cambridge, Mass.: MIT Press, 1999), 435–59, and his paper with Nate Kornell, "Learning Concepts and Categories: Is Spacing the Enemy of Induction?" *Psychological Science* 19 (2008), 585–91.

One of the interesting things about deep practice is that it feels indistinguishable from shallow practice, something Bjork calls the "illusion of competence." Of the several pertinent studies, the most interesting involves British postal carriers who underwent a variety of training methods to learn a new keyboard system. The finding: the postal carriers who learned the least felt they had learned the most, and vice versa. See A. D. Baddeley and D. J. A. Longman, "The Influence of Length and Frequency of Training Session on the Rate of Learning to Type," *Ergonomics* 21 (1978), 627–35.

For more examples of deep practice in advertising, see Jaideep Sengupta and Gerald J. Gorn, "Absence Makes the Mind Grow Sharper: Effects of Element Omission on Subsequent Recall," *Journal of Marketing Research* 39 (May 2002), 186–201.

For insight into improving Shaquille O'Neal's free throws, see R. Kerr and B. Booth, "Specific and Varied Practice of Motor Skill," *Perceptual and Motor Skills* 46 (1978), 395–401.

On Edwin Link and his flight trainer, see Lloyd L. Kelly as told to Robert B. Parke, *The Pilot Maker* (New York: Grosset & Dunlap, 1970); Norman E. Borden, Jr., *Air Mail Emergency 1934* (Freeport, Me.: Bond Wheelwright, 1968); and D. J. Allerton, "Flight Simulation: Past, Present, and Future," *Aeronautical Journal* 104 (2000), 651–63. Good accounts can also be found at http://www.link.com/history.html and Virginia Van der Veer, "Barnstorming the U.S. Mail," *American Heritage*, May 1974.

For more on the skill-building benefits of futsal, see J. D. Allen,

R. Butterly, M. A. Welsch, and R. Wood, "The Physical and Physiological Value of 5-a-Side Soccer Training to 11-a-Side Match Play," *Journal of Human Movement Studies* 31 (1998), 1–11, as well as Simon Clifford's *Play the Brazilian Way* (London: MacMillan, 1999).

CHAPTER 2: THE DEEP PRACTICE CELL

For a good overview of what might soon be called the myelin revolution, see R. Douglas Fields's "White Matter Matters," *Scientific American* (March 2008), 54–61, as well as his "Myelination: An Overlooked Mechanism of Synaptic Plasticity?" *Neuroscientist* 11, no. 6 (2005), 528–31. For an overview of myelin's relationship to diseases and disorders like schizophrenia, obsessive-compulsive disorder, chronic depression, bipolar disorder, autism, dyslexia, and attention deficit hyperactivity disorder, see Fields's "White Matter in Learning, Cognition, and Psychiatric Disorders," *Trends in Neurosciences* 31, no. 7 (July 2008), 361–70. For a more comprehensive education, keep an eye out for Fields's forthcoming book, tentatively entitled *The Other Brain*, to be published by Simon & Schuster.

For specific studies that link myelin to increased skill and talent, see the following: J. Pujol, "Myelination of Language-Related Areas in the Developing Brain," *Neurology* 66 (2006), 339–43; F. Ullen et al., "Extensive Piano Practicing Has Regionally Specific Effects on White Matter Development," *Nature Neuroscience* 8 (2005), 1148–50; T. Klingberg et al., "Microstructure of Temporo-Parietal White Matter as a Basis for Reading Ability," *Neuron* 25 (2000), 493–500; B. J. Casey et al., "Structural and Functional Brain Development and Its Relation to Cognitive Development," *Biological Psychology* 54 (2000), 241–57; K. B. Walhovd and A. M. Fjell, "White Matter Volume Predicts Reaction Time Instability," *Neuropsychologia* 45 (2007), 2277–84; V. J. Schmithorst et al., "Cognitive Functions Correlate with White Matter Architecture in Normal Pediatric Population," *Human Brain Mapping* 26 (2005), 139–47; E. M. Miller, "Intelligence and Brain Myelination: A Hypothesis," *Personality and Individual Differences* 17 (1994), 803–32; and B. T. Gold et al., "Speed of Lexical Decision Correlates with Diffusion Anisotropy in Left Parietal and Frontal White Matter," *Neuropsychologia* 45 (2007), 2439–46.

A sampling of Anders Ericsson's work on deliberate practice can be found in *Cambridge Handbook of Expertise and Expert Performance* (New York: Cambridge University Press, 2006), which he coedited with Neil Charness, Paul Feltovich, and Robert Hoffman; *Expert Performance in Sports* (Champaign, Ill.: Human Kinetics, 2003), which Ericsson coedited with Janet L. Starkes; and *The Road to Excellence* (Mahwah, N.J.: Lawrence Erlbaum Associates, 1996). A fine overview can also be found in his article, coauthored with Neil Charness, "Expert Performance: Its Structure and Acquisition," *American Psychologist* 49, no. 8 (1994), 725–47; and in Michael J. A. Howe, Jane W. Davidson, and John A. Sloboda, "Innate Talents: Reality or Myth," *Behavioral and Brain Sciences* 21 (1998), 399–407.

Not quite as crucial, but nevertheless entertaining, is the fact that deep practice also works with other species (myelin is myelin, after all). See W. S. Helton, "Deliberate Practice in Dogs: A Canine Model of Expertise," *Journal of General Psychology* 134, no. 2 (2007), 247–57.

CHAPTER 3: THE BRONTËS, THE Z-BOYS, AND THE RENAISSANCE

Juliet Barker's *The Brontës* (New York: St. Martin's Griffin, 1994) does an outstanding job of covering the biographical ground. See also Ann Loftus McGreevy, "The Parsonage Children: An Analysis of the Creative Early Years of the Brontës at Haworth," *Gifted Child Quarterly* 39, no. 3 (1995), 146–53, as well as the illuminating analysis of the Brontës, George Eliot, and Charles Dickens in Michael J. A. Howe's *Genius Explained* (Cambridge, U.K.: Cambridge University Press, 1999).

A colorful account of the early days of the Z-Boys is found in Greg Beato, "Lords of Dogtown," *Spin*, March 1999.

For more on the Renaissance-era guild system, see S. R. Epstein, "Craft Guilds, Apprenticeship, and Technological Change in Preindustrial Europe," *Journal of Economic History* 58, no. 3 (1998), 684–713; and S. R. Epstein, *Wage Labor and Guilds in Medieval Europe* (Chapel Hill: University of North Carolina Press, 1991).

For more on Renaissance apprenticeships, see Andrew Ladis and Carolyn H. Wood, *The Craft of Art: Originality and Industry in the Italian Renaissance and Baroque Workshop* (Athens: University of Georgia Press,

1995); Laurie Schneider Adams, *Key Monuments of the Italian Renaissance* (Boulder, Colo.: Westview Press, 2000); Robert Coughlan, *The World of Michelangelo* (New York: Time-Life Books, 1966); and Charles Nicholl's excellent *Leonardo da Vinci: Flights of the Mind* (New York: Viking Penguin, 2004).

For Mr. Myelin's study that shows why Michael Jordan (and every other athlete who depends on speed) had to retire around age forty, see George Bartzokis, "Lifespan Trajectory of Myelin Integrity and Maximum Motor Speed," *Neurobiology of Aging* (2008), available online through PubMed.

On genes' role in skill, see Richard Dawkins's *The Selfish Gene* (Oxford, U.K.: Oxford University Press, 1976).

There's an interesting story regarding Einstein's surplus of myelin. A substitute pathologist, Thomas Harvey, essentially stole Einstein's brain, then spent his lifetime as its caretaker and parceled it out to several fortunate researchers. The full story is told in Michael Paterniti's terrific *Driving Mr. Albert* (New York: Dial Press, 2000). Marian Diamond was one of those researchers, and in 1985 she performed a comprehensive analysis of key regions from both the left and right sides of the brain. She compared Einstein's brain with identical regions from eleven other control brains of men the same age and found that, when it came to the neurons, the brains were the same. However, when it came to myelin-supporting cells, Einstein's brain had twice as many. See Diamond's "On the Brain of a Scientist: Albert Einstein," *Experimental Neurology* 88, no. 1 (1985), 198–204.

CHAPTER 4: THE THREE RULES OF DEEP PRACTICE

Adriaan de Groot's work can be found in the translated *Thought and Choice in Chess* (The Hague, Netherlands: Mouton, 1965), as well as in Vittorio Busato, "In Memoriam: Adriaan Dingeman de Groot," *Association for Psychological Science Observer* 19, no. 11 (November 2006).

Other good works on chunking include W. G. Chase and H. A. Simon, "Perception in Chess," *Cognitive Psychology* 4 (1973), 55–81; and D. A. Rosenbaum, S. B. Kenny, and M. A. Derr, "Hierarchical Control of Rapid

Movement Sequences," *Journal of Experimental Psychology: Human Perception and Performance* 9 (1983), 86–102.

A useful and entertaining source on Moscow's Spartak Tennis Club is in Peter Geisler and Philip Johnston's documentary film *Anna's Army: Behind the Rise of Russian Women's Tennis* (Byzantium Productions, 2005). For more on the history of Meadowmount School of Music, see Elizabeth A. H. Green, *Miraculous Teacher: Ivan Galamian and the Meadowmount Experience* (self-published, 1993).

On self-regulated learning, see Barry Zimmerman and Dale H. Schunk, eds., *Self-Regulated Learning: From Teaching to Self-Reflective Practice* (New York: Guilford Press, 1998); and Barry Zimmerman, Sebastian Bonner, and Robert Kovach, *Developing Self-Regulated Learners: Beyond Achievement to Self-Efficacy* (Washington, D.C.: American Psychological Association, 1996). On volleyball serves, see Barry Zimmerman and Anastasia Kitsantas, "Comparing Self-Regulatory Processes Among Novice, Non-Expert, and Expert Volleyball Players: A Microanalytic Study," *Journal of Applied Sport Psychology* 14 (2002), 91–105.

It would seem logical, given what we've learned about circuits and skill, that every aspiring expert should specialize early. But, in fact, several studies have shown that early specialization isn't as fruitful as a more broad-based approach, particularly when it comes to sports. While that seems contradictory at first, it makes more sense if you consider athletic skills in the largest sense: circuits of balance, coordination, and body control. Witness the number of world-class athletes who specialized relatively late, among them tennis's Roger Federer and NBA stars Steve Nash, Kobe Bryant (all of whom played soccer), and LeBron James (football). For more see Joseph Baker's "Early Specialization in Youth Sport: A Requirement for Adult Expertise?" *High Ability Studies* 14 (2003), 85–94.

For a clear-eyed look at the contrast between American schools and their counterparts in Japan and Germany, see James W. Stigler and James Hiebert, *The Teaching Gap: Best Ideas from the World's Teachers for Improving Education in the Classroom* (New York: Free Press, 1999); also Robert Hess and Hiroshi Azuma, "Cultural Support for Schooling: Contrasts Between Japan and the United States," *Educational Researcher* 20, no. 9 (1991), 2–8.

For more on deep-practicing babies, see K. E. Adolph, P. E. Shrout, and B. Vereijken, "What Changes in Infant Walking and Why," *Child Development* 74, no. 2 (2003), 475–97. A useful summary of the study appears on Greta and Dave Munger's Cognitive Daily blog: http://science blogs.com/cognitivedaily.

CHAPTER 5: PRIMAL CUES

For more on Gary McPherson's study of ignited musicians, see "Commitment and Practice: Key Ingredients for Achievement During the Early Stages of Learning a Musical Instrument," *Council for Research in Music Education* 147 (2001), 122–27. See also his "From Child to Musician: Skill Development During the Beginning Stages of Learning an Instrument," *Psychology of Music* 33, no. 1 (2005), 5–35, as well as his article with Barry Zimmerman, "Self-Regulation of Musical Learning," in *The New Handbook on Research on Music Teaching and Learning* (Oxford, U.K.: Oxford University Press, 2002), 327–47. McPherson's study isn't over yet—the kids he started with when they were seven are now entering university; some of them have built quite a lot of myelin by now.

For a good look at the field of automaticity, see John Bargh, Ran Hassin, and James Uleman, eds., *The New Unconscious* (New York: Oxford University Press, 2005); and Chris Frith, *Making Up the Mind: How the Brain Creates Our Mental World* (New Jersey: Wiley-Blackwell, 2007). In addition, the Situationist (http://thesituationist.wordpress.com) serves as a compendium of research and discussion on a range of subjects related to automaticity and its societal consequences.

Gregory Walton and Geoffrey Cohen's experiment on the impact of a shared birthday, "Mere Belonging," is not yet published. For more on their work, see "Sharing Motivation," in D. Dunning, ed., *The Handbook of Social Motivation* (forthcoming). For a study illustrating similar effects, where subjects are unconsciously primed to increase their efforts, alter their goals, and improve performance, see G. M. Fitzsimons and J. A. Bargh, "Thinking of You: Nonconscious Pursuit of Interpersonal Goals Associated with Relationship Partners," *Journal of Personality and Social Psychology* 84, no. 1 (2003), 148–64.

Other studies flip the ignition switch the other way—they prime subjects to reduce their effort, intelligence, and achievement. For example, see R. Baumeister, C. Nuss, and J. Twenge, "Effects of Social Exclusion on Cognitive Processes: Anticipated Aloneness Reduces Intelligent Thought," *Journal of Personality and Social Psychology* 83, no. 4 (2002), 817–27.

Marvin Eisenstadt's study of eminent orphans can be found in *Parental Loss and Achievement* (Madison, Conn.: International Universities Press, 1989). Another discussion of this phenomenon appears in Dean Keith Simonton, *Origins of Genius: A Darwinian Perspective on Creativity* (New York: Oxford University Press, 1999). A more general treatment is available in Victor Goertzel et al., *Cradles of Eminence: The Childhoods of More than 700 Famous Men and Women*, rev. ed. (Scottsdale, Ariz.: Great Potential Press, 2004).

CHAPTER 6: THE CURAÇAO EXPERIMENT

Charles Euchner, *Little League, Big Dreams: The Hope, The Hype and the Glory of the Greatest World Series Ever Played* (Naperville, Ill.: Sourcebooks, 2006), provides a vivid look at Curaçao's baseball program.

For a comprehensive and scholarly look at motivation, see Carol Dweck and Andrew Eliot, eds., *The Handbook of Competence and Motivation* (New York: Guilford Press, 2005). For Dweck's study measuring the power of one line of praise, see A. Cimpian et al., "Subtle Linguistic Clues Affect Children's Motivation," *Psychological Science* 18 (2007), 314–16. Dweck is also the author of *Mindset: The New Psychology of Success* (New York: Random House, 2006).

For an insightful read on the power of language, see Po Bronson, "How Not to Talk to Your Kids: The Inverse Power of Praise," *New York*, February 12, 2007.

CHAPTER 7: HOW TO IGNITE A HOTBED

KIPP's story has been covered exceedingly well by several journalists, most particularly Jay Mathews at *The Washington Post* and Paul Tough at *The New York Times Magazine*. For more, see Jay Mathews, *Work Hard, Be*

Nice: How Two Inspired Teachers Created America's Best Schools (Chapel Hill, N.C.: Algonquin Books, 2009).

CHAPTER 8: THE TALENT WHISPERERS

The story of Herman "The Baron" Lamm comes from John Toland's *The Dillinger Days* (New York: Da Capo Press, 1995), and Duane Swierczynski, *This Here's a Stick-Up* (Indianapolis, Ind.: Alpha Books, 2002). (Disappointingly, no linguistic evidence links Lamm's name to the origins of the gangster phrase "on the lam.")

For the larger story of Ron Gallimore and Roland Tharp's experimental school, see their *Rousing Minds to Life: Teaching, Learning, and Schooling in a Social Context* (New York: Cambridge University Press, 1988). We have no shortage of excellent books about John Wooden; from a pedagogical perspective, however, it's hard to match Swen Nater and Ron Gallimore, *You Haven't Taught Until They Have Learned* (Morgantown, W.V.: Fitness Information Technology, 2006); Nater is a former UCLA basketball player. In addition, Gallimore and Tharp updated their original Wooden study in "What a Coach Can Teach a Teacher, 1975–2004: Reflections and Reanalysis of John Wooden's Teaching Practices," *Sport Psychologist* 18, no. 2 (2004), 119–37.

For more on Benjamin Bloom's study of 120 top talents, see *Developing Talent in Young People* (New York: Ballantine, 1985).

EPILOGUE: THE MYELIN WORLD

Of the many good accounts of the battle between Phonics and Whole Language, two that stand out are Nicholas Lemann, "The Reading Wars," *Atlantic Monthly*, February 1997; and Charlotte Allen, "Read It and Weep," *Weekly Standard*, July 16, 2007.

For more information about how baby-brain DVDs slow down vocabulary development, see F. J. Zimmerman, D. A. Christakis, and A. N. Meltzoff, "Associations Between Media Viewing and Language Development in Children Under Age 2 Years," *Journal of Pediatrics* 151, no. 4 (2007), 364–68. For more on the general subject, see A. N. Meltzoff, Alison Gopnik, and Patricia Kuhl, *The Scientist in the Crib: What Early Learning Tells Us About the Mind* (New York: Harper, 2000).

The study on cognitive reserve and aging comes from N. Scarmeas et al., "Influence of Leisure Activity on the Incidence of Alzheimer's Disease," *Neurology* 57 (2001), 2236–42.

For more on Carol Dweck's middle-schooler study, see L. S. Blackwell, K. H. Tvzesniewski, and C. S. Dweck, "Implicit Theories of Intelligence Predict Achievement Across an Adolescent Transition: A Longitudinal Study and an Intervention," *Child Development* 78 (2007), 246–63.

Finally, I relied on a vast field of books about skill and talent. Among the best I number the following. Some are memoirs and biographies, included because they offer such vivid depictions of the skill-building process. They may never use the word *myelin*, but its presence is felt on every page.

John Jerome, *The Sweet Spot in Time: The Search for Athletic Perfection* (New York: Breakaway Books, 1980); Glenn Kurtz, *Practicing: A Musician's Return to Music* (New York: Alfred A. Knopf, 2007); Twyla Tharp, *The Creative Habit* (New York: Simon & Schuster, 2003); John McPhee, *A Sense of Where You Are: Bill Bradley at Princeton* (New York: Farrar, Straus & Giroux, 1965); and Steve Martin, *Born Standing Up* (New York: Simon & Schuster, 2007).

Acknowledgments

It's possible to add up this project in several ways: in calendar pages (two years' worth), in distance traveled (50,000 air miles), or in the number of trouncings I experienced when I optimistically attempted to compete in tennis, math, soccer, and various other activities with some of the planet's most highly myelinated people (who'd have thought cellists would be good at Ping-Pong?). But the most lasting way to measure this book is in the generosity and helpfulness of the people I encountered along the way.

In Moscow, I'd like to thank Elena Rybina, Maya Belyaeva, Vitaly Yakovenko, Michael Gorin, and Shamil Tarpischev. In Curaçao, Frank Curiel, Norval Faneyte, Percy Lebacks, Lucio Anthonia, and Philbert Llewellyn. In São Paolo, Dr. Emilio Miranda, Fernando Miranda, and the excellent Mike Keohane of Soccer Futuro. At Meadowmount Music School, Mary McGowan-Welp, Owen Carman, Skye

Carman, Hans Jensen, Melissa Kraut, and Sally Thomas. At Septien Entertainment Group, Mathew Butler, Remington Rafael, Eric Neff, and Sarah Alexander. At KIPP, Sehba Ali, Steve Mancini, Ana Payes, Michael Mann, Leslie Eichler, and Lolita Jackson. At the Shyness Clinic, Nicole Shiloff and Aziz Gazipura. Other helpful guides included Mary Carillo, John Yandell, Eliot Teltscher, Matt Cronin, Chris Downs, Alexei Tolkachev, Charles Euchner, Michael Sokolove, Kim Engler, and Rafe Esquith. I'd also like to thank Robert Lansdorp and Tom Martinez for being such good sports in every sense of the word.

The first exploration of this topic consisted of an article for *Play: The New York Times Sports Magazine*. I'd like to thank *Play*'s editors, Mark Bryant and Laura Hohnhold, for their radiant intelligence and friendship—and also to point out that we're entering our third decade of working together, which must count for something, myelin-wise. Thanks also to the ever-resourceful Charles Wilson for his top-notch research assistance, and to James Watson, Shan Carter, and Kassie Bracken.

I'm grateful to the many neurologists, psychologists, and scientists who lent their time and expertise, especially Doug Fields, Anders Ericsson, and George Bartzokis. I'd also like to thank Albert Bandura, John Bargh, Geoff Cohen, Deborah Feltz, Dan Gould, Bill Greenough, John Milton, Richard Nisbett, Sam Regalado, Ronald Riggio, Jack Rosenbluth, Jim Stigler, Jeff Stone, Christopher Storm, Greg Walton, Mark Williams, and Barry Zimmerman.

Thanks most particularly to my marvelous editor, Beth Rashbaum, whose enthusiasm, patience, and masterful coaching can be felt on each of these pages; to the splendidly talented Barb Burg and Theresa Zoro, whose early support helped launch this book; and to the always helpful Angela Polidoro. Thanks to my agent David Black, who is to his profession what Michael Jordan is to the NBA, as well as to the rest of his outstanding team, including Susan Raihofer, Antonella Iannarino, Leigh Ann Eliseo, and David Larabell.

Speaking of teams, I was lucky enough to have early drafts of the manuscript benefit from the discerning eye of the superb writer Tom Kizzia, as well as that of Todd Balf, whose editorial acumen is exceeded only by his Nerf basketball skills. Others who helped guide the project in various ways include the superb writer Tom Kizzia, Jeff Keller, Rob Fisher, Jim Klein, Marshall Sella, Mike Paterniti, Vince Tillion, Paula Martin, Mark Brinster, Geo Beach, Maya Rohr, Bill Pabst, Ross Riddle, Mark Newson-Smith, Jeff Rabb, Ken Dice, Bill Bell, Jim Gallagher, the staff of *Salty Kat* magazine, and my fellow Little League coaches Bonnie Jason, Douglas Westphal, and Kenton Bloom. I'd like to thank the master teachers of Anchorage public schools, including Nell Simmons, Pat Jobe, Hope Vig, Nina Prockish, Katie Hannon, Carolyn Crosby, Martha Hershberger, Marilyn Cimino, Gordon Spidle, and Putt Middleton. Special thanks to Tom Bursch, who was there for countless conversations about talent, and who, in the streets of São Paolo, was on the receiving end of a memorable demonstration of world-class pickpocketing skill. (And we thought Ronaldinho had good moves. . . .)

This is one of those projects that makes you appreciate your parents, and I'm lucky to have the world's finest. Thanks, Mom and Dad, for everything.

My brother Maurice helped this book in ways that can't be measured. He honed ideas, unearthed examples, and ignited thinking from start to finish, and did it all with such patience and good humor that I'm beginning to suspect that he understands all this far better than I ever will. I'd also like to thank my children, Aidan, Katie, Lia, and Zoe—you're wonderful, and I love you.

Finally, I'd like to thank my wife, Jen, without whom none of this would have happened, and who remains, after all, the most talented person I've ever met.

Index

Page numbers of illustrations appear in italics.

Adams, Jay, 59, 133
Adventures of Tom Sawyer (Twain), 106–8, 119–20
advertising, 19n
age and aging, 44, 45, 66, 67, 115, 215–16
Airmail Fiasco, 20–21, 23
Alexander, Sarah, 184
Ali, Sehba, 144, 145–48, 152
Alzheimer's disease, 215–16
Aristotle, 54, 127
Armstrong, Lance, 34n
art, 47, 126–27
    craft guilds, 54n, 64–66, 64n
    divinely inspired artist, 54, 54n
    Florence and the Renaissance, 2, 61–66, 126–27, 171
Aruba baseball, 125, 131–32
Athens, Greece, 61, 127
Austin, Tracy, 159
automaticity, 37, 109, 170, 229n

baby-brain DVDs, 209–10
Bailey, Donovan, 115
Banks, David, 61–63
Bannister, Roger, 100, 124n
Bargh, John, 109, 111–12
Barker, Juliet, 56–57
Bartzokis, George, 6, 32–33, 66–68, 88, 114–15, 215–16
baseball, 1
    Aruba, 125, 131–32
    Curaçao, 89, 121–26, 127–31
    Little League coaching (Homer), 218–21
    LLWS, 121–22, 121n, 129, 130
    Martinez's coaching advice, 203
    myelin building and, 47
    Venezuelan academies, 100n
basketball, 18
    China as future hotbed for, 100n
    John Wooden, 167–71, 184–85
Beck, Aaron, 213
Becker, Boris, 126

Beckett, Samuel, 74
Bell, Joshua, 84
Bergman, Ingmar, 49
Bjork, Robert, 18, 19, 92
Bloom, Benjamin, 173–76
Bollettieri, Nick, 99
Bolt, Usain, 115
Borg, Björn, 49
Brady, Tom, 198, 201, 202
brain
    age and, 45, 66–67, 215–16
    astrocytes, 40
    breast-fed babies and IQs, 67
    circuit, 36, 37, 41, 42
    disease/disorders and myelin, 39,
        40, 43n, 44, 215–16, 225n
    Einstein's, 73, 73n, 227n
    glial cells, 73n
    of horses, 68
    impulse speed and, 42, 116, 215
    memory, 49–51
    myelin, 5–6, 7, 30–35, 30n, 38–47,
        66–68
    neurons, 32, 36, 38, 40, 41
    oligodendrocytes, 40, 42, 42–43, 72
    plasticity, 39
    scans of pianists, 40
    synapses, 32, 36, 38, 39, 40, 41, 47
    Useful Brain Science Insights,
        36, 37
    white matter, 38, 39, 40
Brazilian soccer, 14–16, 15n, 24–29
    coaching, 191–95
    deep practice, 15–16
    futsal, 12, 25–28, 27n, 34, 127, 219
    primal cues used in, 149
    sustained and continuous ignition
        for, 127
Brazilian Soccer School, 29
Brontës, The (Barker), 56–57
Brontë sisters, 55–58, 56n, 63
Bryant, Kobe, 228n
Burnett, David, 118
Burrell, Leroy, 115, 116

Cabrera, Ryan, 183
Carman, Owen, 85, 93
Carman, Skye, 90–91, 92n
Cervantes, Miguel, 126
Chaplin, Sydney, 21–22
Chase, Bill, 51
Chen, Tina, 84
chess, 52
    brain circuitry and, 37, 43
    chunking and, 78
    committed practice and, 52, 88
    de Groot's experiment and, 76–77,
        79n, 86
    Ericsson and, 48
    mastery and skill acquisition, 32, 48,
        76, 77
    myelin building and, 47
China, 100n
Cho, Fujio, 211
chunking, 77–87, 170, 207
Clarkson, Kelly, 183
Clemente, Roberto, 123, 128
Clifford, Simon, 24–26, 28–29
coaching. See master coaches
cognitive psychology, 49, 79n,
        212–14
Cohen, Geoff, 109, 110–11
Cole, Bruce, 65
comedy, 113n
Coronel, Fermin, 129
Crawford, John Henry, 86–87
Curaçao baseball, 121–31, 136–37
    average player, 121n
    breakthrough-then-bloom pattern,
        124
    facilities for, 122, 127
    ignition, 122–23, 125, 131–32
    language of motivation, 136–37
    at LLWS, 121–22, 124–25
    matrix of causes for success, 125
    sustained and continuous ignition,
        126–32
    time spent at practice, 89
Curiel, Frank, 123, 127–29

Dai Sijie, 100n
dance, 92
Darwin, Charles, 30, 68, 69n
Davenport, Lindsay, 159
deep practice, 12–14, 114, 224n
   absorbing the whole thing, 80–83
   accelerated learning, 2–5, 84, 93
   airplane emergency demonstration, 17–18
   Brontë sisters and, 56n, 57, 60
   chess, 52, 88
   chunking and, 75–87, 170, 207
   conceptual model, 5, 6, 37, 38, 42, 43, 71, 101, 111
   energy required for, 114, 116
   facial expression, 13, 72
   forming desired behavior, 150–51, 150n
   fruitful imitation, 80–83
   John Wooden and, 167–71, 176
   Link's pilot trainer, 20–24
   long-term commitment and, 102–6
   motivation and (see ignition)
   Mozart and, 52
   paradox of, 18
   Ray LaMontagne's practice strategy, 81–82
   Renaissance craft guilds and, 64–66
   repetition and, 87–89
   signs of, in student, 93
   skateboarding, 58–61
   soccer, 15–16, 25–28, 27n, 60
   specialization vs. broad-based, 228n
   as staggering baby steps, 101
   struggle/mistake-making and, 12–13, 18, 34, 94–95, 209–10
   study groups, 18–19
   sweet spot, 19, 19n, 88, 92–93, 177, 224n
   talent code model, 205, 205–6
   tennis, 52
   Ten-Year rule, 51–52, 72
   three rules of, 74–94
   time spent at practice, 88–89, 89n
   Toyota use of, 150n, 210–11
   Virtual Iraq and, 214
   what deep practice feels like, 86–87, 90–92
   word pairs test, 16–17
de Groot, Adriaan Dingeman, 75–79, 79n, 86
"deliberate practice," 51
Delphos, Whitney, 163–64, 165
Dementieva, Elena, 82, 130n
Diamond, Marian, 73n, 227n
diffusion tensor imaging, 40, 51
Downs, Christopher, 124
Duckworth, Angela, 150
Dudamel, Gustavo, 100n
du Pré, Jacqueline, 43n
Dweck, Carol, 135–36, 217–18

education, 140–55, 165–66, 171–72. See also KEEP; KIPP
   American schools, 228n
   baby-brain DVDs, 209–10
   Finland school system, 208–9
   Japan, 94–95
   reading acquisition, 77–78
   Reading Wars, 206–8
   talent code model and, 206–10
Eichler, Leslie, 151
Einstein, Albert, 73, 73n, 227n
Eisenstadt, Martin, 112–13, 113n, 114, 115n
Ellis, Albert, 212–13
Emerson, Ralph Waldo, 97
Engblom, Skip, 60, 132–35, 138n
Epictetus, 213
Epperson, Mary, 173–75, 177, 195, 196
Ericsson, Anders, 47–53, 79n, 80, 89n, 179n
Esquith, Rafe, 141

Fan Wu, 100n
Federer, Roger, 81, 228n
Feinberg, Mike, 139–43, 182, 219

Fields, Douglas, 32, 34, 35–37, 40,
    41–42, 47
Figueiredo, Vincente, 26
film, 65, 100n, 113n
Finland, 208–9
Fischer, Bobby, 52
Fisher, Donald and Doris, 143
Fonseca, Rolando, 14
football, 85
    birth order of top NFL running
        backs, 116
    Martinez and Oakland Raiders,
        196–204
Foulois, Gen. Benjamin, 21
Freud, Sigmund, 48, 212, 213
Fritz, Catherine, 19

Galamian, Ivan, 83
Gallimore, Ron, 165–71, 177, 178, 184,
    185, 189
Gallwey, W. Timothy, 81n
Galton, Sir Francis, 69n
Gaskell, Elizabeth, 55–56
Gatlin, Justin, 115
genes, 69–71
    Darwin model, 46, 68–69
    myelin waves and, 45
    talent and, 5, 14, 71, 72, 73, 88, 101,
        105, 113, 116, 119, 131, 173,
        227n
genius, 92n
    clusters of, 61–63
    Michelangelo and, 65
    nature/nurture model, 63, 68–69,
        69n
    obsessive deep-practice and, 52–53
    "the rage to master" and, 53
German proverb, 11
golf, 33, 43
    South Korean women, 1–2, 33, 98,
        99, 101, 117
Goodman, Kenneth, 206
Graham, Martha, 92
Greene, Maurice, 115

Greenough, Bill, 39
gymnastics, 78–79

habits, 45
Ha Jin, 100n
Harvey, Thomas, 227n
Hedin, Sven Anders, 47–48
Henderson, Lynne, 212
Himanen, Pekka, 209
Horowitz, Vladimir, 88
Howard, Ron, 65
Howe, Michael, 52, 57
HSE (Holy Shit Effect), 74–75, 77, 79,
    220

ignition, 97–120, 221
    conceptual model for, 111
    Curaçao baseball, moments of,
        122–23
    events that create, 98–102
    if/then proposition for, 111
    KIPP program, 144–55
    language of (verbal cues),
        132–38
    master coaches and, 172–76
    McPherson's graph as picture of,
        104, 105
    mile runners, 100–101, 108
    need for sustained and continuous,
        126–32
    parental cues, 106n
    primal cues, 106–20
    selectivity, 117–20, 130, 130n
    talent code model, 205, 205–6
    teacher's performance, 104–5, 108
    "tiny, powerful" idea, 102–6, 106n
    Tom Sawyer example, 106–8
    Whole Language and, 207–8
imitation, 80–83
impulse speed, 42, 116, 215
Inner Game of Tennis, The (Gallwey),
    81n
IQ, 17, 40, 67, 85, 103, 150, 223n
Islanova, Rauza, 130n

Jackson, Lolita, 146, 152–53, 190–91
James, LeBron, 228n
Japan, 94–95, 191–95, 217
Jensen, Hans, 162–66, 177, 196
Johnson, Calvin, 197
Johnson, Paul, 63
Jones, Andruw, 122–24, 125, 128, 130n, 131–32, 143
Jones, Casey, 23
Jones, Quincy, 113n
Jordan, Michael, 67
Juninho (Osvaldo Giroldo, Jr.), 14, 26–27
Jurrjens, Jair, 129

Kaká (Ricardo Izecson dos Santos Leite), 14
Karkkainen, Kaisu, 208
KEEP (Kamehameha Early Education Project), 165–66, 171–72
Kim, Christina, 101
KIPP (Knowledge is Power Program), 140–55, 190–91, 219
Kitsantas, Anastasia, 86
Klingberg, Torkel, 40
Knowles, Beyoncé, 183
Kournikova, Anna, 82, 98–99, 124n
Kraut, Melissa, 162
Kurtz, Glenn, 92

Lamm, Herman, 160–61, 161n, 200
LaMontagne, Ray, 81–82
Landy, John, 100
language of motivation, 132–38
Lansdorp, Robert, 159, 185, 189, 195, 196n
Leonardo da Vinci, 64
Levin, Dave, 139–43, 182, 219
Lewis, Carl, 115, 116
Life of Charlotte Brontë (Gaskell), 55–56
Link, Edwin Albert, Jr., 21–24
Link's pilot trainer, 22–24, 24n, 33

literature, 1
  Brontë sisters, 55–58, 56n
  China as future hotbed for, 100n
  Shakespearean England, 2, 127
Little League World Series (LLWS), 121–22, 121n, 124, 129, 130
Li Yiyun, 100n
Llewellyn, Philbert, 131
Lovato, Demi, 1, 183
Lynch, Kacie, 186–88, 188n

Magana, Daniel, 153–54
"Magical Number Seven, Plus or Minus Two, The" (Miller), 49–50
Ma Jian, 100n
Mann, Michael, 149
Martinez, Tom, 85, 90–91, 196–204, 219–20
master coaches, 159–95. See also specific teachers
  age and, 178–79
  characteristics, 162–66, 168–76, 178–95
  chunking and slowing down, 85
  coaching love, 172–76
  cognitive therapy and, 213–14
  football, 85
  GPS reflex, 185–89
  as integral to success, 125
  Japanese teachers, 93–94
  lack of fame, 196, 196n
  language and, 132–38
  matrix [experience], 178–84, 200
  as mentors, 203–4
  one universal phrase in, 188
  perceptiveness as the second virtue, 184–85
  studies by Gallimore and Tharp, 165–71
  talent code model, 205, 205–6
  theatrical honesty, 189–91
  why teaching soccer is different than teaching violin, 191–95

Maylock, Mike, 197
McPherson, Gary, 2–5, 102–5, *104*,
    117, 119, 229n
Meadowmount School of Music,
    83–87, 90–91, 94, 106n, 210, 213,
    219
memory
    advertising, 19n
    "channel capacity," 50
    decay, 18
    as living structure, 19
    Miller's theory of limited
        short-term, 49–50
    mistakes, use of, 20
    "muscle memory," 37
    name recalling, 17
    neurons, synapses, and, 39
    word pairs test, 16–17
Michelangelo, 64, 65, 126–27
Miller, George, 49–50
Miranda, Emilio, 27–28, 194n
Miranda, Fernando, 194n
mistakes, 20
    use in acquiring skills, 12–13, 17, 18,
        19, 24, 34, 43, 94–95
    Wooden's teaching and, 170–71
motivation, 97. *See also* ignition
    energizing message for, 111, 127
    flipping the trigger (primal cues),
        106–17
    ignition of passion, 98–102
    language for (verbal cues),
        132–38
    signals providing energy, 114, 116
    sustained and continuous ignition,
        126–27
    the tiny, powerful idea, 102–6
Mozart, Amadeus Wolfgang, 52
multiple sclerosis, 39, 43n
Munch, Edvard, 126
muscles (and myelin), 37, 45–46, 68
music, 104–5
    brain scans of pianists, 40
    deep practice, 2–5, 12, 33, 105

    Linda Septien as master coach,
        179–89
    Mary Epperson as master coach,
        173–75
    Hans Jensen as master coach,
        162–66
    McPherson's experiment, 102–5,
        104, 117, 119
    Meadowmount School, 83–87,
        90–91
    myelin building and, 47
    parental loss and, 113n
    Ray LaMontagne and, 81–82
    success of Opus 118 Harlem Center
        for Strings and ignition, 117–20
    teaching violin, 191–95, 217
    time spent at practice, 89
    Venezuelan classical musicians,
        100n
    Vienna composers, 2
    voice, 1, 47, 179–89
myelin, 30–35, 30n, 38–46
    accelerated learning and, 5–6
    acceleration of neural firing and, 41
    age and, 44, 45, 66, 67, 115,
        215–16
    appearance of, 38, *38*, 43
    breast-fed babies and IQs, 67
    cognitive psychology and, 212
    Cro-Magnon man vs. Neanderthals,
        68
    cross-section of nerve fibers, *31*
    daily practice and, 88
    disease and, 39, 40, 43n, 44, 215–16,
        225n
    Einstein's brain and, 73, 73n, 227n
    in foals, 68
    habits and, 45
    humans as myelin beings, 68, 72,
        221
    increased IQ and white matter, 40
    learning disorders and, 40
    in monkeys, 67
    in non-humans, 226n

phospholipid membrane, 38
pianists' brains, 40
practice approach and acquisition
    of, 74–94
"practice makes myelin," 44
praising effort and, 137–38
principles of operation, 44–45,
    217–18
production of, 7, 42–44, 47, 215–16
rats/Tonka truck experiment, 39
reading skill and white matter
    increases, 40
responsiveness to action, 44
skill and, 33, 36–46, 42, 71–73
skill defined as, 6, 33, 58, 61, 73, 117,
    177–78, 210, 211, 214–15, 216
struggle/mistake-making and,
    12–13, 18, 34, 43, 94–95, 209–10
study of, 47
supporter cells and, 40, 42, 42–43
in teenagers, 66
timing and, 41
as universal, 44
vocabulary development and, 40
what building it feels like, 91–92,
    92n
why teaching soccer is different than
    teaching violin, 191–95
wisdom and, 66
wrapping, not unwrapping, by,
    44–45, 214
Myskina, Anastasia, 82, 130n

Narayannan, Latha and Ajiit, 145
Nash, Steve, 228n
Nater, Swen, 170
nature/nurture model, 63, 68–69, 69n
neurology, 38

Oakland Raiders, 196–204
omega-3 fatty acids, 67
O'Neal, Shaquille, 18
Opus 118 Harlem Center for Strings,
    117–19

Pak, Se Ri, 98, 101
passion, 34, 97–102
Pelé, 14, 15, 15n, 193
Perlman, Itzhak, 84, 193
Pettitte, Andy, 123
pilot training, 20–24
Ponson, Sidney, 125, 131
Poswell, asafa, 115
practice. See deep practice
Preobrazhenskaya, Larisa, 82–83, 101,
    173, 189, 196
primal cues, 106–20
    Bargh experiment, 111–12
    birth order and need to keep up,
        115–17
    future belonging, 106–8, 110–11
    KIPP program, 148–49
    parental loss, 112–15, 113n, 115n,
        133
    scarcity and belonging, 117–20
    Scrooge Principle, 110
    selectivity, 117–19
    Tom Sawyer example, 106–8,
        119–20
prodigy, 11n, 80–81
Public School 233, Brooklyn,
    117–20
Pujol, Jesus, 40

"rage to master," 53
Ramos, David, 84
Reading Wars, 206–8
Renaissance, 61–66
Renwick, James, 2–5
repetition or attentive repetition,
    87–89, 170
Richards, Micah, 29
Robbins, Channing, 164
Robinho (Robson de Souza), 14
Rogers, Carl, 213
Romanian filmmakers, 100n
Romário (de Souza Faria), 14, 27
Ronaldinho (de Assis Moreira), 14,
    27n, 34

Ronaldo (Luis Nazário de Lima), 14, 34
Roosevelt, Franklin Delano, 20
Rose, Leonard, 164
Russell, JaMarcus, 197–204
Russian tennis
  coaching, 82–83, 130n, 189
  ignition of passion for, 98–99, 124, 124n
  imitatsiya, 82–83
  Kournikova and ignition, 98–99, 101
  language of motivation, 136
  players in WTA, 99
  primal cues used in, 149
  selectivity as ignition, 130n
  Spartak Tennis Club and top-ranked players, 82–83, 130n
  tekhnika, 83

Safin, Marat, 82, 130n
Safina, Dinara, 82
Sampras, Peter, 159
Sang Yhee, 163, 165
San Mateo College, 198
savants, 52
Scrooge Principle, 110, 125
self-discipline, 150
self-regulation, 85
Seligman, Martin, 150
Septien, Linda, 179–89, 219
Shiloff, Nicole, 212
shorterclarissa2.mov, 2
Shyness Clinic, 212–14
Simon, Herbert, 49, 51, 79n
Simonton, Dean Keith, 114
Simpson, Jessica, 1, 182–83
skateboarding, 58–61, 132–35
Skateboard Kings (film), 59, 60
skill, 6. *See also* deep practice; talent
  automaticity, 37, 37, 109, 170, 229n
  being born, *42*
  as brain circuits, *36*, 36–37, 41–42, *42*
  character formation as, 154–55

child's age and progression, 75
chunking and, 77–79
confidence-building and, 133
defined as "insulation that wraps neural circuits," 6, 33, 58, 61, 73, 117, 177–78, 210, 211, 214–15, 216
de Groot's experiment and, 76–77
as form of memory, 50
genes and, 70–71, 71n
HSE (Holy Shit Effect), 74–75, 77, 79
ignition as energy for creating, 97
imitation and, 80–83
impulse speed and, 42, 116
master coaches and, 165–66, 177–95
myelin and, 33, 36–46, *42*, 71–73, 191–95
progress in acquisition and level of commitment, 102–5, *104*, 117, 119
reading acquisition, 77–78
snowball effect of perception of self, 104–5
struggle/mistake-making as factor in producing, 12, 17, 19, 24, 34, 43
Skinner, B. F., 48
Small Wonders (film), 117–19
Smith, A. J., 203
Smith, Calvin, 116
Snipes, Jason, 143
soccer
  Brazilian players, 14–16, 24–28, 127
  deep practice, 12
  Simon Clifford's team, 24–25, 28–29
  teaching, 191–95
social-fitness training, 212
social networking, 64
Sócrates, José, 14

South Korean women golfers, 1–2, 33, 98, 101, 108, 117, 124, 136

Spartak Tennis Club, Moscow, 82–83, 89, 130n, 136, 210, 213

Spielberg, Steven, 65

Stenmark, Ingemar, 49

Sweden, 49

sweet spot, 19, 19n, 88, 92–93, 177, 224n

Sykes, Charles, 207

talent, 11, 11n. *See also* skill
  breakthrough-then-bloom pattern, 99–102, 100n, 124, 124n
  daily practice, 88
  Ericsson's study of practice, 51–53
  hours needed, for expertise, 51
  HSE (Holy Shit Effect), 74–75, 79, 220
  idea of unique identity and, 61
  myelin and, 33, 61, 216–17
  nature/nurture model, 63, 68–69, 69n
  passion and persistence and, 34, 97–98
  pattern of skill-acquiring process and, 75
  as a process ignited by primal cues, 119
  talent code model, *205*, 205–6
  Ten-Year Rule, 51–52
  "the rage to master" and, 53
  universal principles, 114

talent code, 5, 7, 53, 97, 175, 176, 206, 207
  applied to aging, 215–16
  applied to business, 210–11
  applied to education, 206–10
  applied to Little League coaching, 218–21
  applied to parenting, 216–21
  applied to psychology, 212–15
  diagram of, *205*, 205

talent hotbed, 1–2, 5, 6, 12, 14, 30n, 33, 34, 46, 72–73, 82–85, 98, 101, 127–31, 136–37, 139, 173. *See also* specific places
  appearance of training ground or facility, 82, 109–10, 127, 149
  breakthrough-then-bloom pattern, 99–102, 100n, 124, 124n
  characteristics of master coaches, 127–29, 162–66, 173–76, 178–95
  deep practice and, 46, 75
  factors/complex signals in, 125, 126, 131
  genius and, 92n
  hours of practice daily and, 88–89
  how to create, 139–55
  HSE factor, 75
  igniting, 101, 125–26, 137, 139–55
  language of affirmation at, 136–37
  matrix of causes for, 125
  need for continuous ignition, 126
  one universal phrase among coaches, 188
  passion and, 97–98
  pattern of, 99–100, 100n
  predicting future, 100n

Teach for America, 139

tennis, 49, 99, 126
  Carolyn Xie as prodigy, 80–81
  master coaches, 82–83, 101, 159, 173, 185, 189
  Russian players, 82–83, 98–99
  Ten-Year, ten thousand hour rule, 52
  WTA, growth of Russian players in, 99

Ten-Year Rule, 51–52, 72, 114, 179n
  pattern of talent hotbeds and, 99–100, 100n

Tharp, Roland, 165–71, 184

Thomas, Sally, 94

Toyota, 150n, 210–11
track and field
    birth-order and 100-meter-dash,
        115–16
    mile runners, 100–101, 108, 124n
Tursunov, Dmitry, 82
Twain, Mark, 106–8
Tzavaras, Roberta, 117

Ullen, Fredrik, 40

Vasari, Giorgio, 54n
Venezuela, 100n
Virtual Iraq, 214
voice (singing), 1, 47, 179–89
volleyball, 86
Vygotsky, Lev, 224n

Wadleigh Secondary School of the
        Performing and Visual Arts,
        117–20
Waiting (Ha Jin), 100n

Walton, Bill, 169
Walton, Gregory, 110–11
Winner, Ellen, 53
Wiseman, James, 211
Wooden, John, 167–71, 176, 177,
        184–85, 195, 196, 219
Woods, Tiger, 33
word pairs test, 16–17
Wuthering Heights (Brontë), 58

Xie, Carolyn, 80–81

Yao Ming, 100n
Yeats, W. B., 139
Youzhny, Mikhail, 82
Yo-Yo Ma, 84

Z-Boys, 58–61, 63, 132–35, 171
Zico (Arthur Antunes Colmbra), 14
Zimbardo, Philip, 212
Zimmerman, Barry, 85–86
Zuckerman, Pinchas, 84